ISIDRO FERRER

aBOUT NOthING

CONTEMPORARY MASTERS
OF GRAPHIC DESIGN

HOAKI

C/ Ausiàs March, 128
08013 Barcelona, Spain
T. 0034 935 952 283
F. 0034 932 654 883
info@hoaki.com
www.hoaki.com
hoakibooks

Isidro Ferrer. About nothing.
Contemporary Masters of Graphic Design

ISBN: 978-84-19220-29-5

Publication © 2022, Hoaki Books, S.L.
© text, Miguel Ángel Pérez Arteaga
© personal images and text: Isidro Ferrer

Authors: Isidro Ferrer and Miguel Ángel Pérez Arteaga
Publishing director: Miguel Ángel Pérez Arteaga
Art director: Miguel Ángel Pérez Arteaga
Translator: Kevin Alan Krell
Cover design: Isidro Ferrer
Studio photographs: Ferrer & Mayor / Alicia Goded
Layout: Batidora de Ideas

DL: B 14250-2022
Printed in Turkey

ISIDRO FERRER

aBOUT NOThING

CONTEMPORARY MASTERS
OF GRAPHIC DESIGN

Isidro Ferrer. Madrid, 1963.

National Design Award

National Illustration Award

AGI member. Alliance Graphique International

Member of the International Poster Design Council BICeBé

Founding member of International Council of Poster Design CIDC

Tenured professor of experimental illustration in the Master's program
in Design and Illustration at UPV (Polytechnic University of Valencia)

He created and for ten years (2006-2016) co-directed
International Courses in design and illustration organized by
the Santa María de Albarracín Foundation in Albarracín, Teruel.

Recently, I attended a magic show for the first time. In a theater.
An International Magic Gala. Among the participants were the world champion
of "mentalism" and the European champion of "close-up magic".

Like everybody else, I had seen magicians livening up children's parties
before. Ones that kids make fun of because their tricks are so easy to figure out.
I don't know why but they remind me of the circus clowns from my childhood.
I had also seen them on television: twinkling stars that make the Statue of
Liberty or a Concorde jetliner full of passengers disappear.

Of course, I sat in a box, on the first floor, on a side strategically located
near the stage.

The show began, and I smiled inside. From where I was, I could see a part
that was hidden from the rest of the audience. I could also see small colored
marks on the stage.

The hour-long show included a series of different bits. I saw mind reading,
levitation and disappearing acts. And without a trace of how they were done.

Magic is also called "illusionism".

When something happens that you can't explain, the best thing to do is to
enjoy it and let yourself be carried away. To transform into the child you once
were. Back to a time when everything that happened to you, everything you
dreamed, was amazing.

I give you Isidro Ferrer.

Welcome to the show.

Isidro Ferrer has an irresistible appeal. Those of us who know him personally are drawn to that rare combination of intelligence, charisma and authenticity. And the same for everyone else. Because his work is an accurate reflection of the way he understands life. For me, this would be a combination of two opposing personalities: that of a media star, which might be a mask, and which could be a substitute for the acting career that he would have liked to have had; and that of a solitary craftsman in his workshop, the cabinetmaker or baker that he also would have liked to have been.

I've mentioned before that I work in design and illustration because one day, I started to notice these eye-catching posters on the walls of my city. I was focused (or rather unfocused) on the world of economics, but soon I was hit with a combination of visual and mental punches that made me look in the other direction and set out on a new path. Suddenly, I was aware of the existence of design and advertising. At first, I thought these fields were as brilliant as those posters. But I soon learned that they had all been created by the same person and that the others continued to be as gray and invisible as they had been up to that time.

Nowadays, we're used to seeing his work, observing how it evolves and transforms in a chameleon-like way, yet nothing compares to the almost hypnotic attraction those early works held for me. At that moment, I became a kind of *groupie* who follows his favorite singer around. I collected the culture brochures he began to design for the University of Zaragoza, the posters for college theater, his first illustrations for the newspaper El País, the graphic work for the series En la Frontera (On the Front); his first book, *La aduana del Semoviente (Semoviente Customs)*, published by the bookshop Cálamo; and his first stories.

The first blow I received was when I learned that an illustrator friend had a collection with more rare pieces than mine, and that he was even a bigger Isidro Ferrer fan than I was. He wasn't only the person I had confided in. Numerous people, some of them important professionals, have confessed to me that they have the same addiction. Sharing an idol with other people makes you feel like less of a freak, yet overnight you stop being unique and special and become just like everybody else.

The second blow came years later, and it hit me even harder: I discovered that I couldn't be Isidro Ferrer.

When you set out to do something following someone else's star, you see everything through the lens of this adoration. You research their sources of inspiration; you analyze their style; and you scrutinize their techniques.

Coming from the world of marketing, I know how important it is to adapt to the audience you want to reach, to speak its language. I think I have a good idea of how to choose the concept that needs to be communicated, only one, which must be transmitted directly and clearly. Isidro has internalized this, and it seems to come to him naturally.

Learning to do this appears to be easy. You just need to analyze his posters and try and take a step back and deconstruct them, as they would say in avant-garde cooking. What did he want to say? How did he reach that conclusion?

It doesn't matter what challenge he sets for himself. He always meets it triumphantly in a surprising way. He doesn't miss. It's impossible to replicate his unique way of telling a story. Still, in recent years, a large number of clones have appeared. Stones, wood and found objects proliferate at an exponential rate. Sometimes it's hard to tell if it's a copy. I know he doesn't like it very much. Yet, this inspires him to explore new terrain.

It couldn't be any other way. Several generations of designers and illustrators, in different countries, have been deeply moved by his work. Thousands of students and professionals have attended his workshops, classes and conferences. Wanting to follow in his footsteps is inevitable.

Sadly, his imitators are limited to the form. It isn't enough to situate an object, centered and occupying the entire space, and a typeface unconventionally. You have to know how to talk to the images, with the ideas, and with what is not seen but intuited. This cannot be learned. I once hoped for this. Yet, when you begin to get a hold on this way of telling a story even slightly, he has already invented a new, unattainable language.

It requires great intelligence, determination, hard work, and unlimited ambition to achieve this kind of mastery. You have to devote as much time as needed to distill the information, searched for in the most unexpected places, and transform it, as required, into whispers or into sharp blows.

Speaking the language of clouds or of birds with broken wings isn't as easy or as glamorous as it seems.

Only in case of emergency

"In case of emergency, put on your life jacket, but remember that it should not be inflated until you have left the aircraft." This is an elegant and concise sentence. There's no room for doubt in its interpretation. And yet, every time I hear it, my mind starts to work. I imagine the people around me screaming, trying to advance along the aisles on the plane, all of them stuck in their inflated life preservers like the Michelin man.

It's important to maintain order. To design is to organize.

How does one design a book about Isidro Ferrer? In an orderly way.

For this reason, this book is divided into blocks, each assigned a concept related to his personality.

And for this reason, each concept is related to texts written by Isidro. Personal texts about the profession and related subjects. Different typefaces, sizes and their placement differentiate and organize them.

A project is thus assigned to each chapter: a graphic design, product or illustration project. These are meticulously organized and always carried out in the same way, from the initial sketches to the final result.

For this reason, Isidro has chosen the soundtrack while images from his studio unify all the chapters.

Can order be imposed on that which defies order? No.

How can what expands and floats be organized on a shelf? It isn't possible.

Instructions for use:
1. Open this book randomly and find the first music proposal that appears.
   Search for it in your music app and start to listen to it.
   Ideally with headphones. Close the book.
2. Open the book randomly and turn to the first of Isidro's texts that you find. Read it slowly. With the music always in the background.
   Close the book.
3. Open the book randomly and turn to the first image that you find.
   Keep looking at it. With the music always in the background.
4. Try and find the connection points between the image, text and music.
5. Use the findings as inspiration. Only in case of emergency.
   9 pieces of music x 45 texts x 200 images = 81,000 possible combinations.

ISIDRO FERRER

aBOUT NOThING

Un-swim
Un-tie
Un-growl
Un-think
Un-organize
Un-wander
Un-walk
Un-investigate
Un-arrange

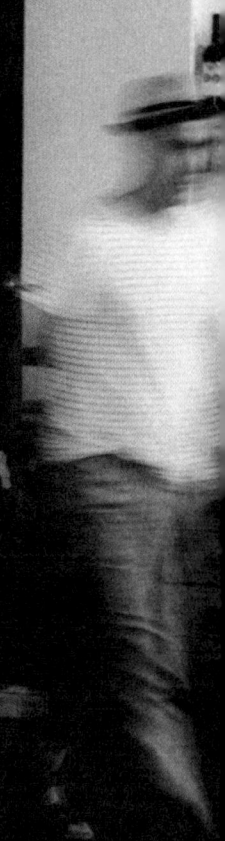

*"What I wanted was to make toys out of words.
To make useless things."*
Manoel de Barros

"The fatigue is as big as this city; 'un-embraceable'. A week without stopping. Tomorrow I begin to return. Today, we rose early to go to the Art Museum with André and Gimena. It hangs miraculously between two red pillars that embrace the body of this cement beast.
The staircase goes into the bowels of the great whale that floats at one end of Paulista Avenue. Its rectangular structure is solidly lightweight.
Lina Bobardi's work is characterized by an emotional purity.

We have lunch at the *buffet*, in front of the huge window that overlooks São Paulo. It's my last day in the city. Constant rain.

We have coffee at Livrería Cultura, a city of books within the city. Everything possesses this city's size: the distances, the waits, the traffic, the *yearning*, the days and the desire. The extraordinary whets the appetite, awakens the senses. Portuguese is a language of whispers. Brazilian is a language of embraces and dance. Next to the café, André places *Book about nothing* in my hands.
He tells me it's one of the most famous works by Manoel de Barros, one of the greatest living poets who write in Portuguese. There's nothing 'unintentional' about the gift. I read out of gratitude. The spell of the words immediately captivates me.

*'As coisas tinham para nós uma desutilidade poética.
Nos fundos do quintal era muito riquíssimo o nosso dessaber'.*

Reading it makes me "retrace" my steps in my memory. Manoel de Barros' 'poetic disutility' leads to childhood; when nothing you say or do, not even what you desire, seeks advantage, profit or gain. The search for pleasure in a pure state defines the first steps of our existence. After that, all effort is concentrated on returning to this state of grace. 'To un-advance'.

The book acts as a compass in my descent towards the poetry of 'un-'.
A poetry built on negation: 'un-use', 'un-knowing', 'un-learning'... The poet knows how to undo the knots that tie words to their meanings and to give them a new life.

*'Un-inventing objects. O pente, por exemplo. Dar ao pente funções de não pentear.
Até que ele fique à disposição de ser uma begônia. Ou uma gravanha.
Usar algumas palavras que ainda não tenham idioma'.*

I aspire to do with design what Manuel de Barros does with words: 'to un-invent it'."

Un-swim

LUNARES

Music
Bebo & Cigala. *Lágrimas negras.*

LUNARES

In 2011, the beer company La Zaragozana decided to overhaul the brand image of Agua de Lunares. The project entailed a global design change ranging from the creation of the logo to graphic communication, including the glass bottle, labels and packaging.

The proposal, which Isidro Ferrer developed in collaboration with Estudio Versus, sought to avoid the use of images and typefaces typical of the sector in order to situate the product in a space of stylistic confrontation with established trends.

The Lunares calligraphic drawing was based on the tests of the first fully geometric typeface that Paul Renner developed for the creation of Futura in 1927.

For the communication campaign, a large-format newspaper was printed. For it, Isidro Ferrer created a series of black-and-white dry-point illustrations to accompany Grassa Toro's poems.

A color version of these same illustrations brightens the back labels of the glass bottles that, soon after publication, became a collector's item.

12 LUNAS • 12 LUNAS
12 LUNAS
MYSTIC POP
JAIME BASULTO_GARAM MASALA
GERMAN DÍAZ
BRIGADA BRAVO&DÍAZ
ANTONIO BRAVO TANGENTES
Jorge Pardo
Tomatito
Mariano Conget
Catherine Vincent
HUMPHREY AND THE FARMERS
NICOLAS SANCHEZ
JOHN COLTRANE
BLUE NOTE
ZAZ
PABLO ESTIGARRIBIA TANGOS PARA PIANO
LOUIS ARMSTRONG Classic Armstrong
FURTHER EXPLORATIONS
Boy Gé Mendes Noite de Morabeza
Marc Parrot
QU'EST-CE QU'ON S'FAIT CHIER!
Ibon Errazkin
SON DE LA FRONTERA
CRISTINA BRANCO
mariza
waiting for the moon
tindersticks

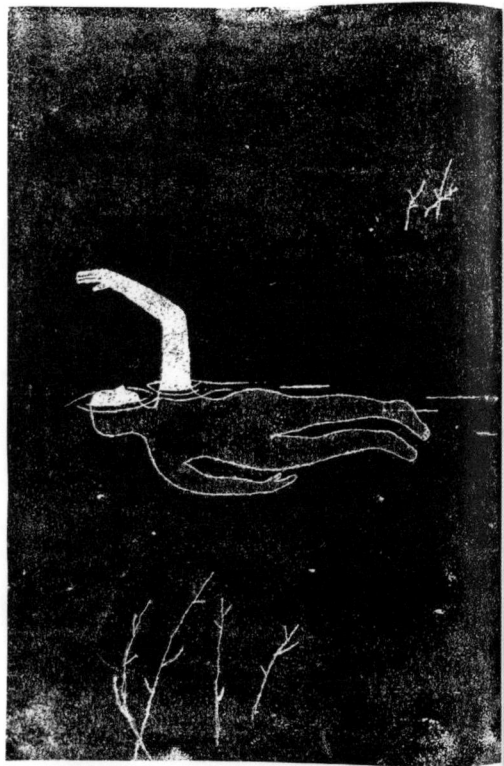

En
una
botella
vacía
cabe
el
sol

En
una
botella
vacía
cabe
la
mano
de
un
hombre
decidido
a
llenarla

"My father was from Villareal de los Infantes, a town in the province of Castellón. My grandfather had a clothing and fabric store there. He also had a country house on the outskirts of the city and some land.

My father's only brother inherited the orange-tree fields. On my first visit to my grandparents' house that I remember, we went to spend Sunday at my aunt and uncle's little farmhouse in Burriana. The house was barely more than a hut where they kept the farm equipment, set between the orange trees and a long thin pebble beach. We ate paella. After the paella, the adults dozed in the shade. I took advantage of their siesta to get lost among the orange trees. I must have been 6 or 7 years old. Just enough for fear not to stifle my curiosity. I don't remember how long I was playing among the trees. It couldn't have been much time. The voice of my parents calling my name summonsed me back to reality.

—Isidro! Isidrooo!

I returned to the beach running. There I found my parents and my aunt and uncle waist-deep in the sea.

—Isidro! Isidrooo! —They were shouting frantically. None of them knew how to swim. I froze. They couldn't see me because they had their backs to me. In the middle of the sea, a shape was floating at the mercy of the waves. It was a dark medium-size shape, perhaps a trunk.

—Isidro! Isidrooo!

The shape was bobbing up and down, appearing and disappearing between the waves. Terrified, I thought:

—If the one afloat in the middle of the sea is Isidro, then who am I?"

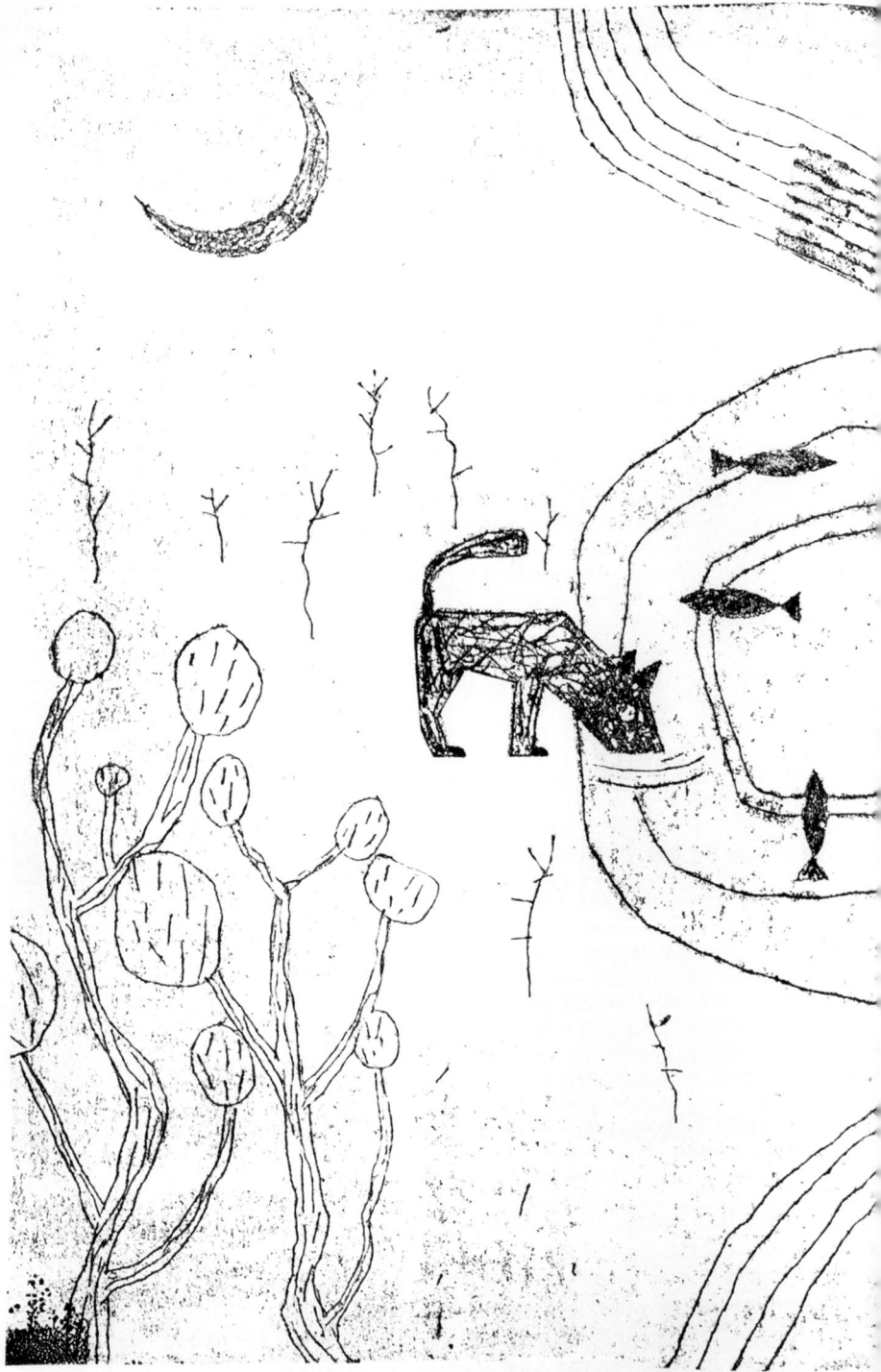

"When I talk about myself, I feel like I'm talking about someone else, about the other.

Rimbaud said, 'I am other'. Schopenhauer went further when he said, 'I am others'. In the same vein, I look for ways to dissolve into everyone else.

I studied theater arts to perfect the art of division without having to suffer from dissociative identity disorder or schizophrenia. For years, I worked as a professional actor. I switched to graphic design when I realized that in the theater, to be others you need an audience to confuse. In illustration, I found a way to get closer to the goal of evaporation by departing from the invisibility that working alone provides.

In a way, illustration allows me 'to be others'. And it does this through the use of 'representation', one of the instruments of creation that, while still very much present in the performing arts, takes on a more precise dimension in illustration. To represent is 'to make something present with words or shapes that the imagination retains; to be an image or symbol of something, or to imitate it perfectly.'

I embrace representation as a way to comprehend the world, to organize and express it, to connect, through action, objects with words."

"Homage is recognition. We recognize in others parts of the whole that are common to us, and unknown parts of an accessible whole. To recognize is to be aware of the known and to assign it the value needed for it to stay fixed in our memory.

John Berger points out that, 'What's visible exists because I've seen it before'. This being aware of the visible for 'having seen it before' is what shapes and sustains memory. I recognize because I remember. But recognizing is not only moving closer to what is outside oneself to discover its identity and nature. To recognize is also to be grateful, to admit and accept the traces that others leave behind in oneself."

Un-tie

CDN

Music
Jun Miyake. *Lost Memory Theatre.*

CDN

In 2006, the National Drama Centre (CDN) renewed its graphic communication image, entrusting the project to Isidro Ferrer. The collaboration lasted for eight seasons. During this time, Isidro designed 120 posters.

Gerardo Vera, the Center's director for the first five seasons, became a partner in crime on this adventure. He urged the designer to transform the graphic image of the CDN into something more than merely an advertising opportunity. He pushed him, from a well-reasoned position, to endow the images with the semantic value needed to ensure that each poster was a unique piece of work that would remain in the viewer's memory.

Despite the conceptual unity that runs throughout the series, each differs from the previous due to an aesthetic change. For this, Isidro Ferrer used different resources to create a recognizable, coherent and homogeneous graphic structure.

After a two-year hiatus, the new director, Ernesto Caballero, entrusted him again with the design. The only condition was that he would not repeat any of the aesthetic arguments used in previous seasons. The designer found the solution in the use of exclusively typographic elements.

Design created in collaboration with Nicolás Sánchez (2006-07 and 2007-08 seasons) and Sean Mackaoui. (2008-09 seasons).

CENTRO DRAMÁTICO NACIONAL
DIRECCIÓN
GERARDO VERA

TEMPORADA
20
08
/
20
09

TEATRO
MARÍA GUERRERO
TEATRO
VALLE-INCLÁN

CENTRO DRAMÁTICO NACIONAL
DIRECCIÓN: GERARDO VERA

TEMPORADA
2007 / 2008
TEATRO MARÍA GUERRERO
TEATRO VALLE-INCLÁN
http://cdn.mcu.es

Centro
Dramático
Nacional

Centro
Dramático
Nacional

TEMPORADA   2014   / 2015

Teatro
María Guerrero
Teatro
Valle-Inclán

Centro
Dramático
Nacional

TEMPORADA   2015 | 2016

Teatro
María Guerrero
Teatro
Valle-Inclán

"I don't know how to define myself. Sometimes I'm an illustrator of concepts and others one of emotions.

I know that ideas, concepts, grant prestige to illustration. They make it shine. But I also know that emotion makes it heart beat, makes it sensual.

Light or shadow, idea or emotion, that's the biggest dilemma I face on a daily basis.

To be cerebral or to do it compulsively. To proceed with discipline and order or to do it from the gut, spontaneously and unrestrained."

"The great Robert Massin, the French graphic artist, typographer and creator of the graphic interpretation of The Bald Soprano by Eugène Ionesco published by Éditions Gallimard in 1964, liked to reiterate the closeness between the scenic arts and design. Massin did it from the vantage point of language. He established an etymological relationship between the functions of theater direction (mise en scène) and publishing design (mise en page).

On several occasions, I've been asked about the importance of theatrical training in my graphic work. Until recently, I wasn't very aware of this influence, nor had I really thought about it. But after working for seven seasons on creating the graphic component of the National Drama Center, I recognized this connection as something essential to the way I approach graphic design.

Two crucial hermeneutic elements unite theater and design: performance and representation. A circular dance between idea and reality that shapes knowledge. Both theater and design demand performing and representing, and to make performance and representation a creative expression.

In a poster for a play, the different voices that make up the dramatic core are interpreted and represented: the author's voice, the director's voice, the voice of the actors. In both cases, in theater and design, the work is based on the voice of others.

My role as a designer is to find the right register to interpret and represent on paper the essence of the scenic performance. To give a voice to others. To be the other voice."

UN ENEMIGO DEL PUEBLO

de **Henrik Ibsen**

**Centro
Dramático
Nacional**

**Teatro Valle Inclán
del 25 de enero
al 25 de marzo
de 2007**

Versión
Juan Mayorga
Dirección
Gerardo Vera

**Centro
Dramático
Nacional**

PRESAS
de **Verónica Fernández**
e **Ignacio del Moral**

Dirección
Ernesto Caballero

Teatro Valle-Inclán

**Del 22 de noviembre
al 30 de diciembre
de 2007**

Centro
Dramático
Nacional

ANTE LA JUBILACIÓN
de **Thomas Bernhard**

Traducción
Miguel Saénz
Dirección
Carme Portaceli

Teatro Valle-Inclán
Sala Francisco Nieva
del 21 de febrero
al 6 de abril
de 2008

Centro Dramático Nacional

REY LEAR
de **William Shakespeare**

Versión
Juan Mayorga
Dirección
Gerardo Vera

**Teatro María Guerrero
del 14 de febrero
al 20 de abril
de 2008**

Centro
Dramático
Nacional

URTAIN
de **Juan Cavestany**

Dirección
Andrés Lima

**Teatro Valle-Inclán
del 25 de septiembre
al 2 de noviembre
de 2008**

**Centro
Dramático
Nacional**

HAMLET
de **William Shakespeare**

Dramaturgia
**Borja Ortiz de Gondra
Juan Diego Botto**
Dirección
Ernesto Caballero

Teatro María Guerrero

**Del 4 de diciembre
de 2008
al 4 de enero
de 2009**

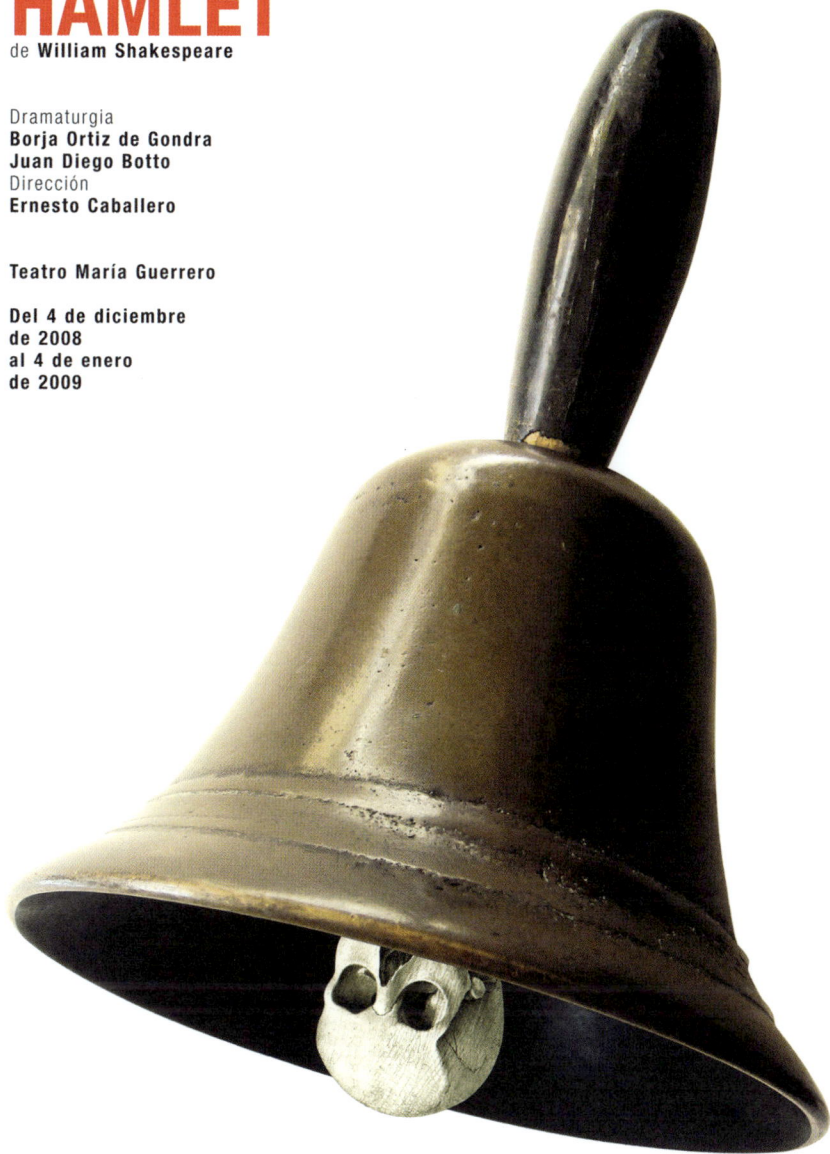

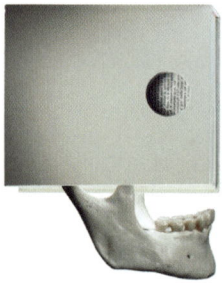

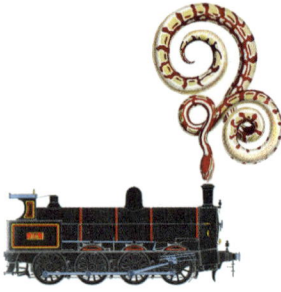

Centro
Dramático
Nacional

PLATONOV
de **Anton Chéjov**

Versión
Juan Mayorga
Dirección
Gerardo Vera

Teatro
María Guerrero

desde
el 19 de marzo
al 24 de mayo
de 2009

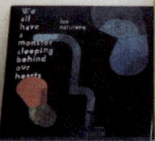

"If the artist's tradition is to transform into somebody else, the designer's is to transform into everybody else.

The mask, which simultaneously covers (hides) and reveals (shows), helps in this virtuous function of transformation.

To lie is to transform reality and shed light on the reality of fiction. The lie is one of the possible paths for creation. Even more, I'll be so bold as to say there is no creation without deceit. Lying and invention require a fervent imagination to build possible realities."

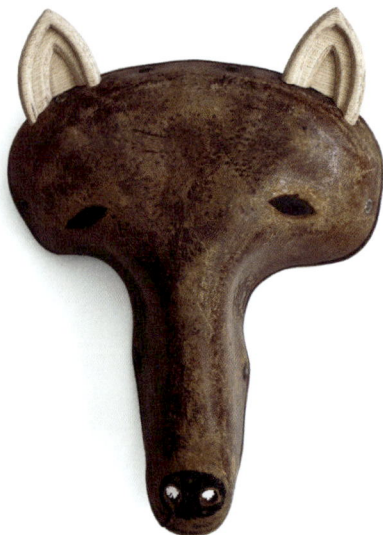

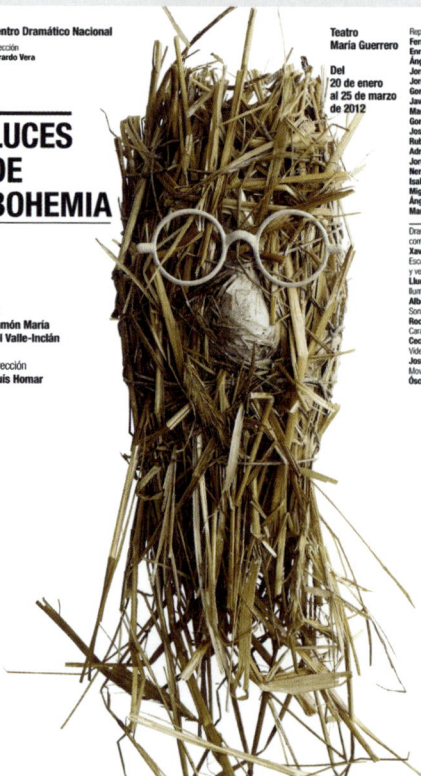

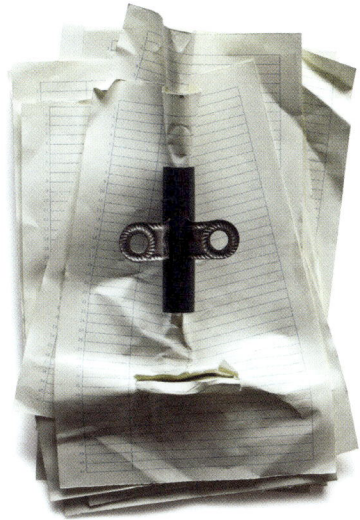

Centro Dramático Nacional
Dirección
Gerardo Vera

Teatro
Valle-Inclán

Del
7 de diciembre
de 2011
al 19 de febrero
de 2012

Reparto
Amparo Baró
Sonsoles Benedicto
Alicia Borrachero
Irene Escolar
Gabriel Garbisu
Antonio Gil
Carmen Machi
Markos Marín
Miguel Palenzuela
Chema Ruiz
Clara Sanchís
Marina Seresesky
Abel Vitón

Escenografía
Max Glaenzel
Vestuario
Alejandro Andújar
Iluminación
Felipe Ramos
Sonido
Roc Mateu
Videoescena
Álvaro Luna

AGOSTO (Condado de Osage)
de
Tracy Letts

Versión
Luis García Montero
Dirección
Gerardo Vera

Centro Dramático Nacional
Dirección
Gerardo Vera

Teatro
María Guerrero
Sala
de la Princesa

Del
2 de diciembre
de 2011
al 15 de enero
de 2012

Reparto
Pilar Massa
Goizalde Núñez

Versión
Lucy Collin
Escenografía y vestuario
Rafael Garrigós
Iluminación
Francisco Ariza

Producción
Carallada Show
Prem Teatro

CONTRAACCIONES
de
Mike Bartlett

Dirección
Pilar Massa

Centro Dramático Nacional
Dirección
Gerardo Vera

Teatro
Valle-Inclán
Sala
Francisco Nieva

Del
11 de noviembre
al 23 de diciembre
de 2011

Reparto
(por orden alfabético)
David Castillo
Carmen Conesa
Adolfo Fernández
Teresa Lozano
Macarena Sanz
Samuel Viruela
Ileana Wilson

Escenografía
Paco Azorín
Vestuario
Ikerne Giménez
Iluminación
Luis Perdiguero
Diseño de sonido
y música
Luis Miguel Cobo
Vídeo
Emilio Valenzuela
Eduardo Moreno

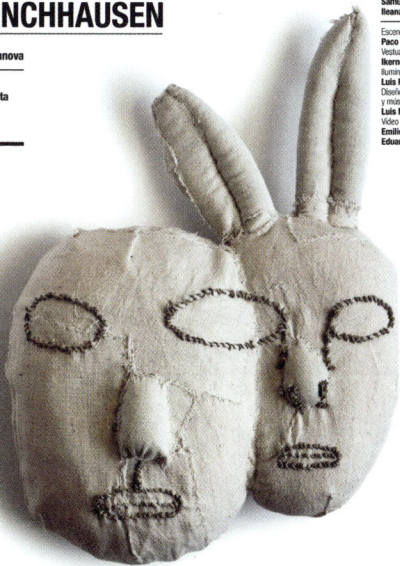

MÜNCHHAUSEN
de
Lucía Vilanova

Dirección
Salva Bolta

Centro Dramático Nacional
Dirección
Ernesto Caballero

Teatro
Valle-Inclán
Sala
Francisco Nieva

Del
13 de enero
al 19 de febrero
de 2012

Reparto
Daniel Muriel
Eleazar Ortiz
Helio Pedregal

Versión
Mauro Armiño
Escenografía y vestuario
Alejandro Andújar
Iluminación
Albert Faura

LA MECEDORA
de
Jean-Claude Brisville

Dirección
Josep Maria Flotats

"Humor is an attitude towards life that can lead to art.

Art, and poetry is one of the many forms that art takes, is useless, and it is because it's impractical. But this lack of usefulness is its highest function. Art and humor save human beings because they free us from the seriousness of life.

Humor is based on the absurd and the tragic nature of existence. It subverts conventional categories and appropriates them for the realm of comedy while simultaneously revealing a hidden version of reality poetically.

Through metaphor, humor and poetry reveal the innate duality in all things. They take us out of ourselves. They allow us to see the pitfall of everything, to understand that everything has a downside and that everything can be different from what we understand it to be."

Centro Dramático Nacional

Dirección
Ernesto Caballero

Teatro
María Guerrero
Sala
de la Princesa

Del
17 de abril
al
17 de junio
de 2012

Festival
Internacional
de
Títeres

7
espectáculos
para
niños
de
3 a 100
años

TITIRIMUNDI

Centro Dramático Nacional

Dirección
Ernesto Caballero

TI
TERE
SCE
NA

**De septiembre de 2014
a mayo de 2015**

”Not too long ago, a design student at a respected college let me
know, point-blank and out of the blue, that in a class exercise in which
the students had analyzed one of my posters, they had reached the
conclusion that, unfortunately, my work wasn't up to snuff.
Apparently, my poster deviates from some of the essential
fundamentals of design and, specifically, typography.
　　—That's true, I answered her. I'm sure you're right.
I wasn't lucky enough to study design. My language is based on comic
strips, misses and errors. Since I'm not beholden to the arbitrariness
of academic orthodoxy, I have to rely on intuition. In contrast to the
infallibility that knowledge of the rules provides, intuition doesn't
guarantee correctness. I appreciate your sincerity. Next time,
I'll try and do better.”

AZAR

Centro Dramático Nacional
Dirección
Ernesto Caballero

Teatro
María Guerrero
Del
5 al 23
de noviembre
de 2014

EL JUEGO DEL AMOR Y DEL AZAR

Reparto
(por orden alfabético)
Enric Cambray
Àlex Casanovas
Rubén de Eguia
Guillem Gefaell
Vicky Luengo
Bernat Quintana
Mar Ulldemolins

de
Pierre de Marivaux

Dirección
Josep María Flotats

Escenografía
Ezio Frigerio
Iluminación
Albert Faura
Vestuario
Franca Squarciapino

Centro Dramático Nacional
Dirección
Ernesto Caballero

LA PECHUGA DE LA SARDINA

Teatro
Valle-Inclán
Sala
Francisco Nieva

Del
25 de febrero
al
29 de marzo
de 2015

de
Lauro Olmo
Dirección
Manuel Canseco

Reparto
(por orden alfabético)
Manuel Brun
Marta Calvo
Jesús Cisneros
Víctor Elías
María Garralón
Nuria Herrero
Marisol Membrillo
Cristina Palomo
Amparo Pamplona
Natalia Sánchez
Juan Carlos Talavera
Alejandra Torray

Escenografía
Paloma Canseco
Iluminación
Pedro Yagüe
Vestuario
José Miguel Ligero
Espacio sonoro
Roberto Cerdá

Centro Dramático Nacional
Dirección
Ernesto Caballero

Teatro
Valle-Inclán

Del
21 de noviembre
de 2014
al
11 de enero
de 2015

FAUSTO

Dirección
Tomaž Pandur

Versión
Tomaž Pandur,
Lada Kaštelan
y Livia Pandur

Reparto
(por orden alfabético)
Manuel Castillo
Víctor Clavijo
Roberto Enríquez
Alberto Frías
Emilio Gavira
Antonio Gil
Aarón Lobato
Rubén Moscato
Pablo Rivero
Marina Salas
Ana Wagener

Escenografía
Sven Jonke
Iluminación
Juan Gómez Cornejo
Vestuario
Felype De Lima
Vídeo
Dorian Kolundzija
Música
Boris Benko, Primož Hladnik

Centro Dramático Nacional
Dirección
Ernesto Caballero

Teatro
María Guerrero
Sala
de la Princesa

Del
15 de abril
al
17 de mayo
de 2015

ADEN TRO

de
Carolina Román

Dirección
Tristán Ulloa

Reparto
(por orden alfabético)
Nelson Dante
Araceli Dvoskin
Noelia Noto
Carolina Román

Escenografía
Alexandra Alonso
Vestuario
Clara Bilbao
Iluminación
Eduardo Alonso Chacón
Música
Julio de la Rosa

Centro Dramático Nacional
Dirección
Ernesto Caballero

Teatro
María Guerrero

Sala
de la Princesa

Del
30 de octubre
al
29 de noviembre
de 2015

BANG-KOK

Texto y dirección de
Antonio Morcillo López

Reparto
Carlos Álvarez-Nóvoa
Dafnis Balduz

Escenografía
Paco Azorín
Vestuario
Gimena González Busch
Iluminación
Kiko Planas
Espacio sonoro
Ramón Ciércoles
Caracterización
Toni Santos

Producción
La Villarroel,
Grec 2015 Festival de Barcelona

Centro Dramático Nacional
Dirección
Ernesto Caballero

Teatro
Valle-Inclán

Del
20 de noviembre
2015
al
10 de enero
2016

LOS HERMANOS KARAMÁZOV

de
Fiódor Dostoievski

Dirección
Gerardo Vera
Versión
José Luis Collado

Reparto
Juan Echanove
Óscar de la Fuente
Fernando Gil
Markos Marín
Antonio Medina
Antonia Paso
Marta Poveda
Lucía Quintana
Chema Ruiz
Ferran Vilajosana
Eugenio Villota
Abel Vitón

Escenografía
Gerardo Vera
Iluminación
Juan Gómez-Cornejo
Vestuario
Alejandro Andújar
Música y espacio sonoro
Luis Miguel Cobo
Videoescena
Álvaro Luna

Centro Dramático Nacional
Dirección
Ernesto Caballero

Teatro
Valle Inclán

Sala
Francisco Nieva

Del
23 de septiembre
al
1 de noviembre
de 2015

REIKIAVIK

Texto y dirección de
Juan Mayorga

Reparto
Daniel Albaladejo
Elena Rayos
Cesar Sarachu

Escenografía y vestuario
Alejandro Andújar
Iluminación
Juan Gómez Cornejo
Imagen
Malou Bergman
Sonido
Mariano García

Producción
Entrecajas Producciones Teatrales

Centro Dramático Nacional
Dirección
Ernesto Caballero

ASÍ QUE PASEN CINCO AÑOS

de
Federico García Lorca

Dramaturgia y dirección
Ricardo Iniesta

Reparto
(por orden alfabético)
Elena Amada Aliaga
Jerónimo Arenal
Manuel Asensio
Carmen Gallardo
Silvia Garzón
José Ángel Moreno
María Sanz
Raúl Sirio Iniesta
Raúl Vera

Espacio escénico
Ricardo Iniesta
Composición musical
Luis Navarro
Dirección coral
Esperanza Abad
Vestuario
Carmen de Giles
Maquillaje
Manolo Cortés
Coreografía
Juana Casado
Diseño de luces
Miguel Camacho

Teatro
Valle-Inclán

Del
1 de abril
al
15 de mayo
2016

"The theater poster is the prologue of the work. Through the image, it introduces us to the dramatic piece. But the poster also is the epilogue, what is fixated in the memory after the performance.

The poster comes before the performance; after the performance, the poster remains."

TEATRO MARIA GUERRERO
CENTRO DRAMATICO NACIONAL
Centro Dramático Nacional
Dirección
Ernesto Caballero
Temporada
016 _
2017
Teatro
María Guerrero
Teatro
Valle-Inclán
inaem
http://cdn.mcu.es

Un-growl

PETIT THÈÂTRE. LAUSANNE.

Music
Pascal Comelade. *Le Primitivisme.*

PETIT THÈÂTRE. LAUSANNE.

In 2019, Le Petit Théâtre de Lausanne updated its graphic communication image. The theater, located in an old building in the historic city center, is thirty years old and its list of shows consists of works exclusively for children.

For Isidro Ferrer, the work became a gift that enabled him to combine his three great passions: theater, graphic expression and childhood.

Haydé Ardalan, an illustrator of Iranian origin and creator of the well-known cat Milton, has been in charge of the Swiss institution's graphic image for twenty years. The posters she has made during this time are populated by a personal universe filled with felines and birds. Isidro Ferrer suggested a drastic change in form, though one that was ultimately respectful, maintaining the animal presence as one of the graphic storylines. More than a change, he saw it as an evolution.

During this time, the seasonal communication elements were gradually modified, including the programming and production posters, the corporate image and the signage of the physical space of the Theater.

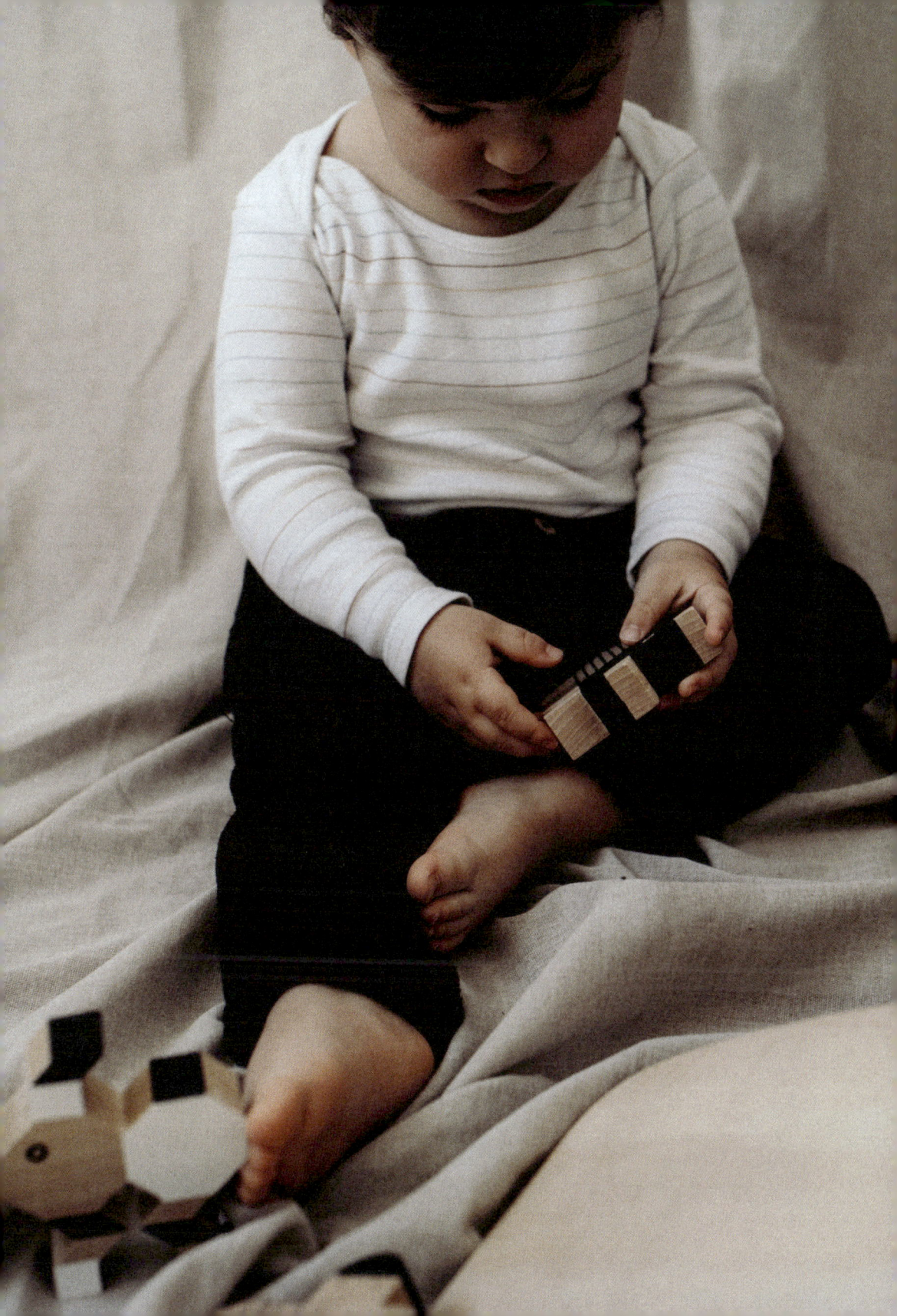

Du 4 au 15 mai 2022

Être le loup

Par Collectif les chts de l'asphAlte

Tout public dès 6 ans

LE PETIT THÉÂTRE LAUSANNE

Tout Bêtement

LE PETIT THÉÂTRE LAUSANNE

Par la Cie Cantamisù

Tout public dès 5 ans

LE PETIT THÉÂTRE LAUSANNE

The Divine Company

Du 2 au 31 décembre 2020

Tout public dès 7 ans

alice, Retour aux merveilles

PLACE DE LA CATÉDRALE 12
CH-1005 LAUSANNE
lepetittheatre.ch

LE PETIT THÉÂTRE
LAUSANNE

Par les
arTpenteurs

Tout
public
dès
6 ans

Le Rêve de Nehemo

Du
21 avril
au
9 mai
2021

PLACE DE LA CATEDRALE 12
CH - 1005 LAUSANNE
021 323 62 13
lepetittheatre.ch

"Illusion is an indissoluble part of graphic design, for two reasons: because our raw material consists of the concepts, images and representations that originate in the imagination, and because one of the purposes of our work is to inspire hope. In this sense, I like to think of graphic design as a kind of optical illussionism."

"I've never had a pet. The few birds and the only fish we had at home to brighten our kids' childhood ended their days tragically (best not to go into details).

I've never felt the need to have a pet. I'm allergic to cats and dogs locked up between four walls, and birds stuck in cages make me very sad.

I prefer images of animals. I understand image not only as the prints that illustrate a book but as any reality that occurs more than thirty feet away. My relationship with animals is exclusively reflective and aesthetic.

On the other hand, I've come to realize that over the years, my graphic universe has become increasingly populated by eccentric and omnipresent wildlife that grow in size and importance. I took on some professional assignments (Camper for kids, Funny Farm, LZF Lamps) using elements typical of fables, although, in contrast to the recurring use of zoology, my illustrations have neither a didactic purpose nor a moral. In my work, animals and things have a rhetorical and/or aesthetic function.

Some animals recur insistently in my imagination. They inhabit my notebooks and are the focus of many of my creations. Monkeys and elephants are at the top of the pyramid of my favorites, followed by rabbits, deer, all kinds of birds, felines, equines and reptiles. On the other hand, other animals don't grab my attention in the least. These tend to be domestic animals, mostly dogs and cats, though cows and sheep as well. Chickens are another story. While they are domestic, chickens have also awoken my curiosity and sympathy.

Maybe I don't know how to draw human beings, or maybe the animal world lends itself more to transformation and nonsense. I don't know."

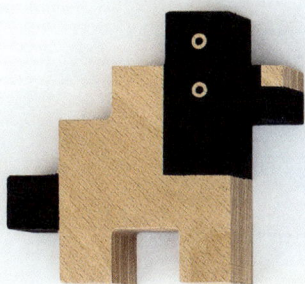

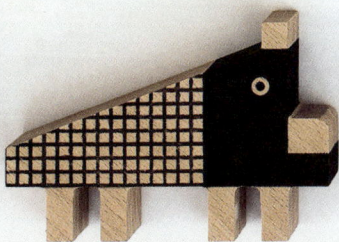

LE PETIT THÉÂTRE LAUSANNE

GROU!
11 au 19 septembre 2021
Cie Renards / Effet Mer
dès 7 ans

C'EST TES AFFAIRES!
25 septembre au
3 octobre 2021
Création / Reprise
Cie Predüm
dès 5 ans

UNE LUNE ENTRE DEUX MAISONS
9 au 17 octobre 2021
La Manivelle Théâtre
dès 3 ans

RŪNA
3 au 21 novembre 2021
Création
Cie STT
dès 6 ans

**SEULE DANS
MA PEAU D'ÂNE**
2 au 20 février 2022
Création
Cie Face Public
dès 7 ans

A BÂTONS BATTUS
13 au 23 janvier 2022
Theater De Spiegel
dès 1 an

ALICE, RETOUR AUX MERVEILLES
1er au 31 décembre 2021
Création / Reprise
The Divine Company
dès 7 ans

À TABLE!
5 au 13 mars 2022
L'Arrière-Scène
dès 3 ans

saison

2021
2022

MIRANDA, REINE DE QUOI?
16 au 27 mars 2022
Cie du Théâtre du Loup
dès 6 ans

LA BARBE
26 et 27 février 2022
Jerrycan et Speaker B
dès 3 ans

FRACASSE
30 mars au 3 avril 2022
Cie des Ô
dès 8 ans

DES YEUX POUR TE REGARDER
6 au 13 avril 2022
Méli Mélodie
dès 3 ans

ÊTRE LE LOUP
4 au 15 mai 2022
Création
Collectif les cRis de l'asphAlte
dès 6 ans

Place de la Cathédrale 12
CH - 1005 Lausanne
+ 41 (0)21 323 62 13
lepetittheatre.ch

"The Star" is a bar where every night, a strange and varied menagerie of picturesque characters from Huesca, the city where I live, meet. Each one has their story written on their face. They laugh and drink in earnest. It's an archaic and nocturnal bohemia whose denizens, in spite of the obvious passing of time, keep their dignity.

Serafín is a regular. He is a painter who has the entire dictionary in his head and who constructs his speech whimsically, piecing together scattered fragments from the encyclopedia.

One Friday, after a few beers, Serafín sat down next to me. He looked at me wordlessly, with intense seriousness. After a while, he said:

—You know what your problem is, Isidro?

—No. I have no idea. Tell me, Serafín, what's my problem?

—The feeling of nothing has taken root in you, and the nothing is very contagious. It spreads quickly. Nothing immediately fills everything with nothing. An excess of nothing is as harmful as the absence of it. You have to have the right amount of nothing. The necessary nothing.

After a brief silence, he continued.

—One of these days, I'm going to go and see the eye of the world. Maybe I'll take you with me...

—That would be nice, Serafín. When are we going? I asked him practically beaming.

As if he hadn't heard my response, he grew silent again and after a long pause, said:

—No, Isidro. You absolutely cannot come with me. You wouldn't know how to appreciate it."

septembre

GROU! C'EST TES AFFAIRES!

lu	ma	me	je	ve	sa	di
		1	2	3	4	5
6	7	8	9	10	11	12
13	14	15	16	17	18	19
20	21	22	23	24	25	26
27	28	29	30			

automne
lundi du jeûne fédéral

octobre

C'EST TES AFFAIRES! UNE LUNE ENTRE DEUX MAISONS

lu	ma	me	je	ve	sa	di
			1	2	3	
4	5	6	7	8	9	10
11	12	13	14	15	16	17
18	19	20	21	22	23	24
25	26	27	28	29	30	31

vacances
halloween et heure d'hiver

novembre

RŪNA

lu	ma	me	je	ve	sa	di
1	2	3	4	5	6	7
8	9	10	11	12	13	14
15	16	17	18	19	20	21
22	23	24	25	26	27	28
29	30					

décembre

ALICE, RETOUR AUX MERVEILLES

lu	ma	me	je	ve	sa	di
		1	2	3	4	5
6	7	8	9	10	11	12
13	14	15	16	17	18	19
20	21	22	23	24	25	26
27	28	29	30	31		

saint-nicolas et hanoukka
noël
vacances
hiver
saint-sylvestre

janvier

À BÂTONS BATTUS

lu	ma	me	je	ve	sa	di
				1	2	
3	4	5	6	7	8	9
10	11	12	13	14	15	16
17	18	19	20	21	22	23
24	25	26	27	28	29	30
31						

vacances
fête des rois

février

SEULE DANS MA PEAU D'ÂNE LA BARBE

lu	ma	me	je	ve	sa	di
	1	2	3	4	5	6
7	8	9	10	11	12	13
14	15	16	17	18	19	20
21	22	23	24	25	26	27
28						

nouvel an chinois
chandeleur
saint-valentin
vacances

mars

À TABLE MIRANDA, REINE DE QUOI? FRACASSE

lu	ma	me	je	ve	sa	di
1	2	3	4	5	6	
7	8	9	10	11	12	13
14	15	16	17	18	19	20
21	22	23	24	25	26	27
28	29	30	31			

printemps
heure d'été

avril

FRACASSE DES YEUX POUR TE REGARDER

lu	ma	me	je	ve	sa	di
				1	2	3
4	5	6	7	8	9	10
11	12	13	14	15	16	17
18	19	20	21	22	23	24
25	26	27	28	29	30	

vendredi saint
lundi de pâques
vacances

mai

ÊTRE LE LOUP

lu	ma	me	je	ve	sa	di
						1
2	3	4	5	6	7	8
9	10	11	12	13	14	15
16	17	18	19	20	21	22
23	24	25	26	27	28	29
30	31					

fête du travail
fête des mères
l'ascension

LE PETIT THÉÂTRE
LAUSANNE

Seule
Dans ma
peau
d'âne

Du
2 au 20
février
2022

Tout
public
dès
7 ans

Cie
Face public

Mise en scène
Sophie Gardaz
et
Michel Toman

PLACE DE LA CATEDRALE 12
CH - 1005 LAUSANNE
021 323 62 13
lepetittheatre.ch

"In my work, strangeness is the point of departure, contradiction the point of arrival. Along the way, I take the implausible and the absurd that appears in the guise of the real to give each thing its hidden form."

LE PETIT **THÉÂTRE**
LAUSANNE

Par Cie STT
Super trop top

Du
octobre
au
novembre
2021

Tout
public
dès
6 ans

Rûna

Secret,
murmures
et magie

PLACE DE LA CATEDRALE 12
CH - 1005 LAUSANNE
021 323 62 13
lepetittheatre.ch

"A father walks along a street in Zaragoza holding the hand of his daughter, who is just over two years old. In the middle of the road, a disemboweled bird is stuck to the asphalt like a piece of gum.

—Look, Dad, a dead bird, the girl observes without a hint of tragedy in her voice.

—No, dear. It's asleep, her father corrects her in a high-pitched voice."

t

2022-23

SEPTEMBRE

**UN PETIT AIR
DE CHELM
CACHE-CACHE
WOUAH!**

lu	ma	me	je	ve	sa	di
			1	2	3	4
5	6	7	8	9	10	11
12	13	14	15	16	17	18
19	20	21	22	23	24	25
26	27	28	29	30		

lundi
du jeûne
fédéral   automne

OCTOBRE

lu	ma	me	je	ve	sa	di
					1	2
3	4	5	6	7	8	9
10	11	12	13	14	15	16
17	18	19	20	21	22	23
24	25	26	27	28	29	30
31						

vacances

heure
d'hiver

halloween

**WOUAH!
SINUS ET DISTO**

NOVEMBRE

lu	ma	me	je	ve	sa	di
	1	2	3	4	5	6
7	8	9	10	11	12	13
14	15	16	17	18	19	20
21	22	23	24	25	26	27
28	29	30				

toussaint

LILOLA

DÉCEMBRE

LITTLE NEMO

lu	ma	me	je	ve	sa	di
			1	2	3	4
5	6	7	8	9	10	11
12	13	14	15	16	17	18
19	20	21	22	23	24	25
26	27	28	29	30	31	

saint-nicolas

hiver

vacances   noël

hanouka

saint-sylvestre

JANVIER

**TOIICI & MOILÀ
OZ**

lu	ma	me	je	ve	sa	di
						1
2	3	4	5	6	7	8
9	10	11	12	13	14	15
16	17	18	19	20	21	22
23	24	25	26	27	28	29
30	31					

fête des rois

vacances

nouvel an
chinois

FÉVRIER

**OZ
TOUT BÊTEMENT**

lu	ma	me	je	ve	sa	di
	1	2	3	4	5	
6	7	8	9	10	11	12
13	14	15	16	17	18	19
20	21	22	23	24	25	26
27	28					

chandeleur

vacances

st-valentin

MARS

**TOUT BÊTEMENT
SOUS UNE PLUIE D'ÉTÉ
LES FRÈRES CHOUM
L'ŒUF**

lu	ma	me	je	ve	sa	di
	1	2	3	4	5	
6	7	8	9	10	11	12
13	14	15	16	17	18	19
20	21	22	23	24	25	26
27	28	29	30	31		

chandeleur

printemps   heure d'été

AVRIL

**L'ŒUF
LA POMME
EMPOISONNÉE**

lu	ma	me	je	ve	sa	di
					1	2
3	4	5	6	7	8	9
10	11	12	13	14	15	16
17	18	19	20	21	22	23
24	25	26	27	28	29	30
31						

vendredi
saint

vacances

lundi de
Pâques

aïd el-fitr

MAI

**LA POMME
EMPOISONNÉE**

lu	ma	me	je	ve	sa	di
1	2	3	4	5	6	7
8	9	10	11	12	13	14
15	16	17	18	19	20	21
22	23	24	25	26	27	28
29	30	31				

fête
du travail

fête
des
mères

ascension

lundi de
pentecôte

CAMPER

to float

Un-think

CAMPER

Music
Mulatu Astatke. *New York-Addis-London.*

CAMPER

In 2012, Isidro Ferrer began to collaborate with the shoe company Camper. The first assignment was to create the window display decals for the store to advertise Sales. The following year, they asked him to design their Christmas display decals.

For this, he created the figure of an anthropomorphic rabbit that is the focus of different graphic and volumetric applications.

In 2015, Camper decided to overhaul its "Camper for kids" brand image. A humorous ant tap dancing with the new logo on its trunk is the motif for the shoe boxes, promotional poster and some merchandising elements. From then on, for two years, Isidro Ferrer was responsible for creating the images to promote the different seasons.

The seasonal posters created as part of this communication campaign won the BICebé First Prize at the Bolivia Poster Biennial.

ME
RRY

CHRIST
MAS

CAMPER
for
kids

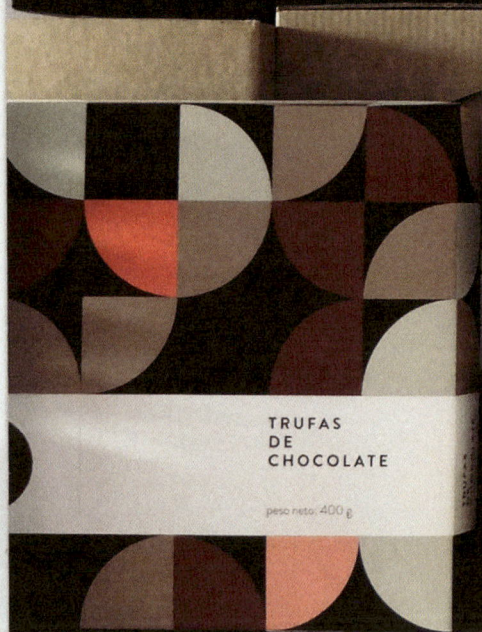

TRUFAS
DE
CHOCOLATE

peso neto: 400 g

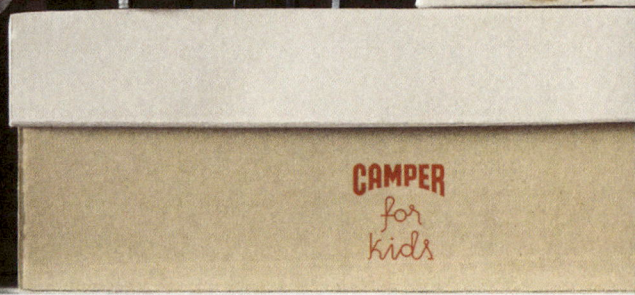

CAMPER
for
kids

ASCASO

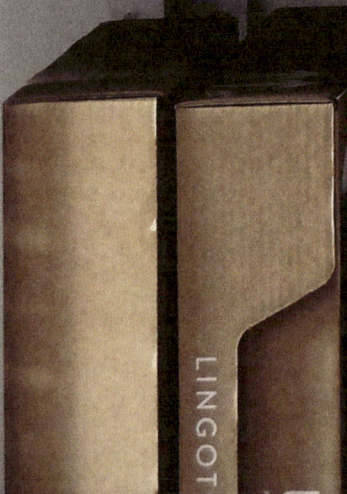

LINGOT

Lo'a

PASTAS DE TÉ

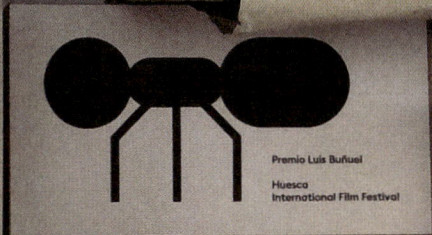

Premio Luis Buñuel

Huesca
International Film Festival

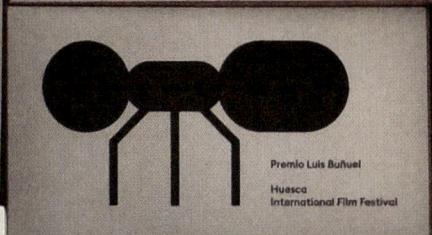

Premio Luis Buñuel

Huesca
International Film Festival

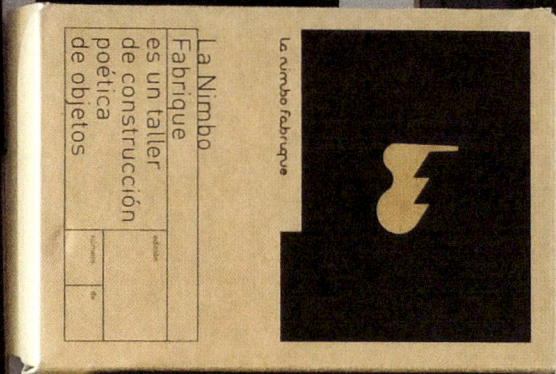

La Nimbo
Fabrique
es un taller
de construcción
poética
de objetos

la nimbo fabrique

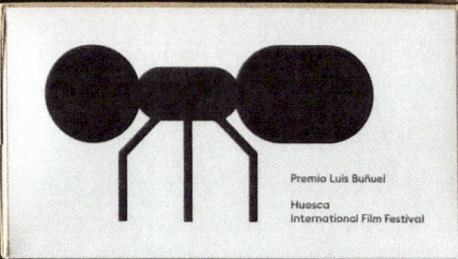

Premio Luis Buñuel

Huesca
International Film Festival

lzf

OPEN HERE

"Lying is one of the purest acts of creation. Beyond the burden of moral guilt that it unjustly entails, lying has enormous transformational power. To lie is to invent, to imagine, to pretend, to act; to lie is to create.

We lie for a multitude of different reasons: to hide, to deceive, to avoid taking responsibility, to obtain a benefit, or to hurt someone. But we also lie to fantasize, to build, to unveil, to seduce.

We know that the clergy and the political class lie, but writers, actors, scientists, poets and designers do too.

Lying is an incredibly efficient and versatile tool for arriving at imaginary solutions."

21

22

23

Alaró

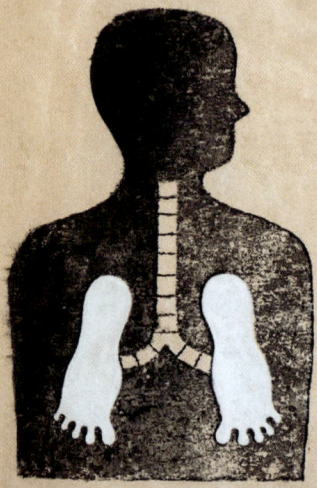

EL LABERINTO ES UNA METÁFORA.
EL LABERINTO ES UNA INVITACIÓN A LA BÚSQUEDA,
A RESOLVER EL ENIGMA DEL RECORRIDO.
CADA PASO SE MUEVE EN EL INTERIOR DE UN
LABERINTO. CADA NUDO ES UN LABERINTO.
CUANDO SE SALE DEL LABERINTO NUNCA SE
VUELVE AL LUGAR DE ORIGEN.

C

"To be creative is not a state of grace. It's a forced routine. Stopping and looking is a step; greeting the unexpected is another.

We shouldn't confuse creativity with inspiration. Creativity comes from within; inspiration comes from without. We have to work at creativity; for inspiration, we have to wait. Inspiration is the excuse of lazy people and the refuge of the amateur."

"For some time, I've approached my work with the persistence of the inevitable, as a triumphal fatalism, a heroic and joyful resignation. What thing?

Things accumulate. This is one of the properties of things: accumulation and the randomness of the accumulation. Yes, things accumulate. They accumulate one on top of the other creating mountains of things.

In these arbitrary piles, single entities and singularity are blurred and end up merging into an abstract cluster of junk.

Things arrive, occur, appear, accumulate. I rigorously try to impose order, rank, and reason on them. Everything has its place, I tell myself. And everything has its time. I inherited these strategies from my father, though his method has eluded me. He was determined to provide me with good rules of conduct.

For some time now, I don't control many of the things that happen to me. I hardly even decide. I just let them pass by. I let them pass me by.

It happens with tasks, with work. Sometimes I lose perspective. I don't know how to situate myself geographically over the things I have to do. I do, and by doing I eliminate the anguish of accumulation. But in spite of this effort, in spite of my daily determination to clear the horizon to locate the four compass points and identify elements to help orient me, nothing I have opened or begun is completed or is specified. I don't reach the end of the things. This isn't out of apathy or laziness but because of that modern sickness called 'multitasking': everything at once; nothing in its place.

Multitasking is the best weapon against efficiency. Now I know it: I become ineffective as a result of dullness, as a result of accumulation. And thanks to this daily tangled mess of obligations, of sensations, of emotions, I am losing the ability to rejoice. Instead of celebrating what happens, I want what's happening to end so I can move on to something else. The stuff of madmen..."

"I'm a traveling medicine man peddling miracle hair growth elixir. Every day I lie more. Every day I lie better. Is lying deceitful? Is lying an art?

I return from another performance and I lie as always, with a feeling of shame, almost of disgrace, and with the same old question. Does this public exhibition have any purpose? This vain demonstration of work?

I convince myself (to quiet the beast) that this theatricalization of the craft is alien to me, that it's in others and that learning comes from sharing processes and experiences.

Yes, that' s it. I tell myself.

Yet despite this benevolent reading to reassure myself, I know that I'm part of the farce, of this almost circus-like spectacle, of the even more difficult one, into which we are turning this profession. It's no longer enough to work, and to do it honestly within the silence of one's studio. Now we have to shout from the rooftops so everyone will hear of the goodness and excellence of each of our achievements.

Respectable audience. Come and see the amazing visual spectacle of graphic design."

Mary W. Shelley

Traducción **Antonio Méndez Rubio**

Ilustraciones **Isidro Ferrer**

FRaN kenS tein

Un-organize

FRANKENSTEIN

Music
Glend Gould. *Bach: The Goldberg Variations.*

FRANKENSTEIN

In 2021, the Image Research and Development Center of the University of Castilla-La Mancha asked Isidro Ferrer to take on the publishing design assignment for a new translation, led by Antonio Méndez Rubio, of *Frankenstein, or The Modern Prometheus, by Mary W. Shelley.*

In an attempt to be as faithful as possible to the romantic context of the story, to capture the phantasmagoric essence of the monstrous creature that Dr. Frankenstein brings to life, to illuminate the psychological complexity of the novel and to reflect the baroque nature of the landscape descriptions, Isidro Ferrer drew on the "super marionette" theory and decided to build a changing set of sceneries in which to place the characters.

He constructed the scenes with the aim of highlighting humankind's unbalanced relationship with the nature of events. A mise en scène emerges where geometry and abstraction create enveloping atmospheres inspired by the work of Adolphe Appia and Gordon Craig: a play of lights and shadows that, like German Expressionist cinema, projects a deformed reality that invites the reader to participate dramatically in the reading of the book.

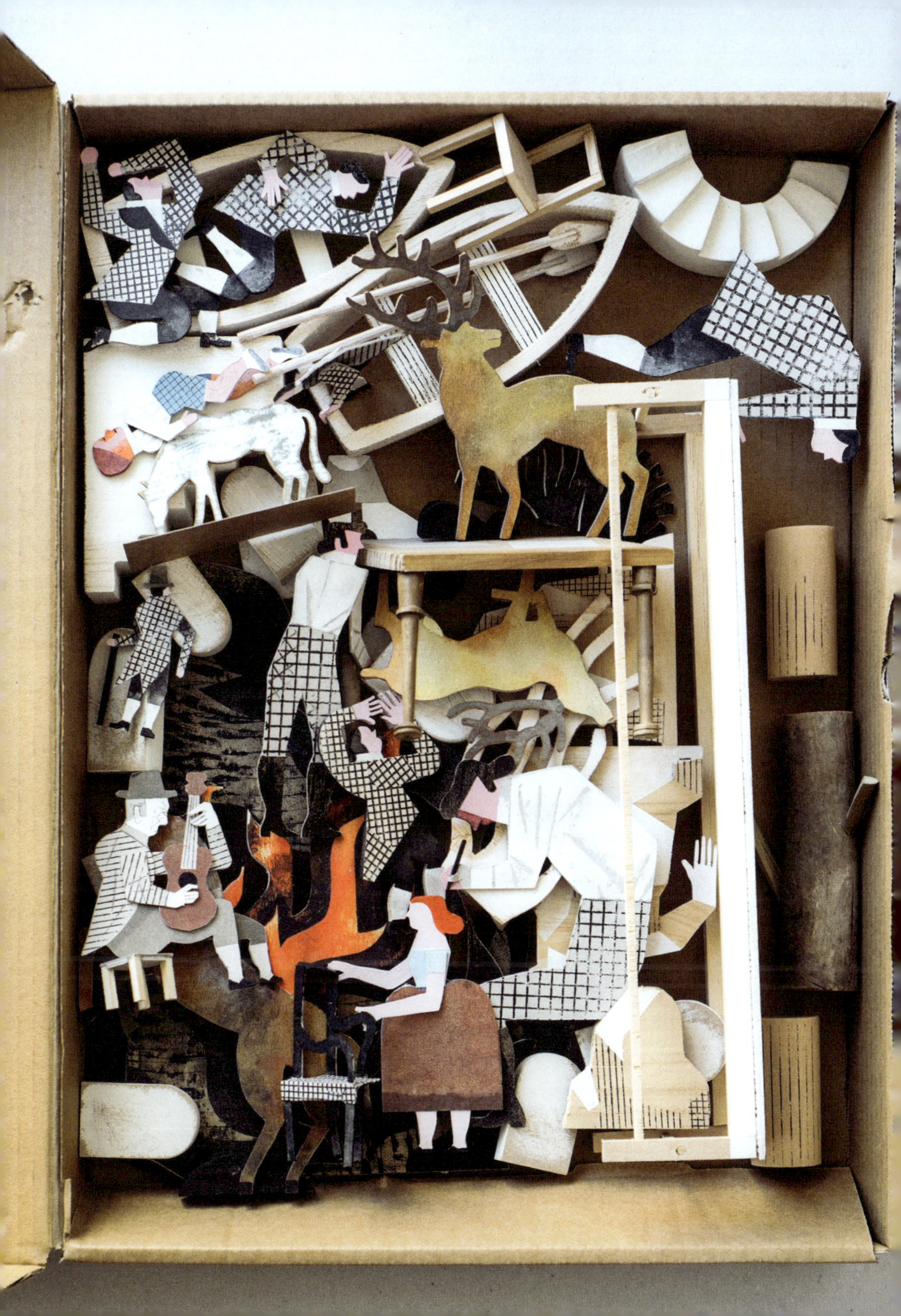

"Disorder is a way to activate one's surroundings. Disorder makes it possible to find unexpected solutions, what Orson Welles called 'divine accidents', the Surrealists 'objective chance', and Jung 'synchronicity'.

In my case, disorder is a work methodology that allows me to integrate what is unprecedented into the creative process, although I try to make disorder be a harmonious disorder, not an invalidating disorder."

"The overall din in the universe of images is guaranteed because the image is substituting words in the field of communication. The proliferation of emoticons exemplifies this.

There are more and more images that say nothing. Images of full and empty plates, images of kittens, images of sunsets, images to stroke the ego or to mask loneliness, images to demand constant attention, images, images...

In this chaotic bustle of visual noise, everything gets confused. Nothing gains relevance or uniqueness.

Even though an image in its original form is intelligent and useful, as soon as it exits the communication space for which it was intended and is churned up by the digital blender, it loses its meaning and becomes visual *fast food*.

Graphic design bears some responsibility for this idiotic and insubstantial verbiage of visual banality."

The soul

"In the entrance to Café del Alma, there's a sign that says, 'Food made with love, breakfast with soul'. Curiosity is stronger than my rejection of bad taste. I eat my breakfast waiting for a miracle that never occurs.

What use is a soul without a body?, the Czech poet Vladimir Holan wondered.

Juan de Dios, my neighbor on Concepción Arenal Street in Zaragoza, a magician apprentice and medical student, asked the professor in his first anatomy class where the soul was located in the human body, provoking laughter from his peers.

Certainly none had read the Czech poet or understood the scope of the question. Nor did Juan de Dios. Yet without knowing it, he was reclaiming the corporeality of ideas and feelings."

"Delving into the inner workings of things, into the fragility of language, turning over the skin of objects, losing oneself on the back side of the paper, flowing over the blank white front page, learning to see to observe, learning to observe to understand, closing one's eyes to look ahead, opening them to look sideways, staying alert and attentive to the unexpected, granting the possibility of existing to chance, searching and finding, not throwing away what is unusable because it's useless, losing oneself in disorder, questioning and questioning oneself, questioning not only the 'how' but also the 'what', the 'why', asking each name what it wants to be called, asking each object what it wants to be, achieving balance on the spine of uncertainty, doubting methods, doubting certainties, not being the same every day, honing the words until the right one is found, letting oneself be swept up by the current, going against the current, amassing hope with patience, cultivating strangeness, keeping wonder alive, the excitement burning, feeling sensations by simply imagining them, doing, undoing, doing it again."

IMITAR
ASIMILAR
INNOVAR

DENIS SCHMITZ
DIRECTOR DE COMUNICACIÓN
HERMÉS

REUNIÓN EN SEPTIEMBRE

PHILIP CARTER - ENVÍO "HOMBRES CONTADOS"

YALU FRANKEL - OPEN EVERY DAY

CEDILIJ - MARIANA GONZÁLEZ

Un-wandering

LOS SUEÑOS DE HELENA

Music
Naná Vasconchelos. *Saudades.*

LOS SUEÑOS DE HELENA

Los sueños de Helena (Helena's Dreams), published by
Libros del Zorro Rojo in 2021, Is a book in which Uruguayan
writer Eduardo Galeano records the dreams that his wife
Helena tells him every morning.

To be faithful to the dream material with which Galeano
worked and to play with the same liquid tools of memory,
Isidro Ferrer found his best ally in a process of un-closeness.

After reading the text closely, several times, almost to the
point of memorizing it, he set it aside and nearly forgot it.
After a long time and without re-reading the original text,
Isidro Ferrer recalled the story solely from memory. This is
how he created the illustrations based on the abstraction
of memory. As a result, the images don't correspond to
what the words evoke but rather to what the memory of the
words arouses.

VIVIR es existir dentro de una concepción del tiempo, pero recordar es abandonar esa noción de tiempo. Todos los recuerdos por muy remotos que sean tienen lugar "ahora", en el momento en el que la mente los rememora.

Cuanto más se recuerde algo, más oportunidades tiene el cerebro de refinar la experiencia original. Porque todo recuerdo es recreación, no reiteración.

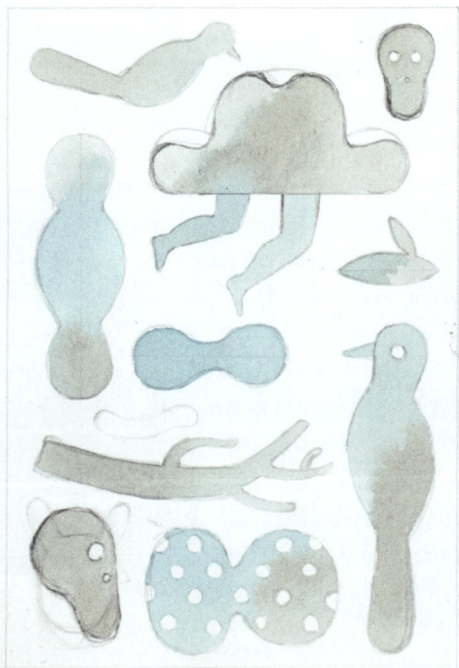

"To the question, 'What is poetry?' Nicanor Parra, the Chilean poet of 'anti-poetry', responded: 'Poetry is everything that moves, what changes place'.

This affirmation that endows the physical phenomenon of movement with intellectual and emotional capacity is related to the ideas of Henry David Thoreau and Robert Walser. It encourages me to look for a kind of poetic stance in displacement."

"Moving, changing place, going from here to there, roaming. Walking is a way of claiming what is local in that it guarantees the experience of stepping on the site and maintaining direct contact with it. But walking isn't only going. It's also to consider the return. Walking can be the way to make the journey of turning back, of the descent until 'finding the place'. This way of advancing to retreat, of growing to diminish is a purifying process of elimination of the superfluous that lies in the celebration of the place and in uniqueness."

"September has the name of beginning. September sounds like a door half-open, the rustle of leaves. September smells like a blackboard and chalk, a new book, freshly printed letters.

September has the name of an invisible city. You can stroll along its streets without the intention of arriving anywhere. September has veiled colors and the slight smell of wood.

A month to cultivate intentions, to kiss the afternoons, to walk on tiptoes, to open umbrellas, to open pores and squint one's eyes.

September takes me back to the years of short pants and skinned knees. Almonds, figs and blackberries collected at the base of a tree.

You can only live in September one month a year."

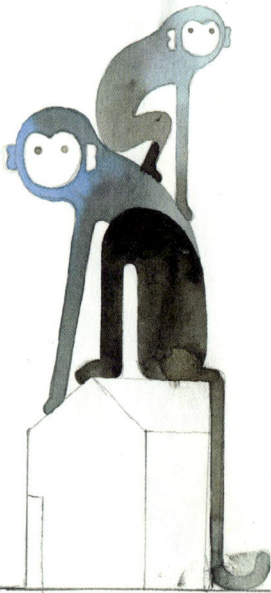

"I kicked off September with a new notebook in which to draw and write. It's the closest thing to the thrill of starting a new book and burying one's nose in the aroma of printed ink. This new notebook, like the ones before it, isn't intended for drawing. It fell into my hands by accident. I shy away from notebooks made for drawing. They frighten and immobilize me; they're too demanding. I prefer notebooks that rebel against their use and set their own capricious rules.

I run my hands along the paper. It returns imperfection to me like an offering. I like flawed beauties, unique in their tiny imperfections. When I start a notebook, I get a giddy feeling of vertigo. All choices are available on its blank pages; its emptiness harbors the desired whole, an imagined whole.

Hesitantly, respectfully, I stain the first pages. The pencil opens fissures of shadow on the white landscape of the paper. The first drawings are imbued with a mixture of fear and modesty. Erring confirms my human condition. In each notebook I try to encourage chance."

FERIA DE TEATRO - 25 aniversario
Teatro, Danza, nuevas espacios escénicas.
Medados de Abril.

JUEVES

- CIBELES → RESPONDER A ...   EMPTY - CAJA
- WEB AYUNT Z...
- RECOGER MATE...
- RESPONDER SA...
- VIAJE CON C...

La tristeza pudo más que la resistencia.

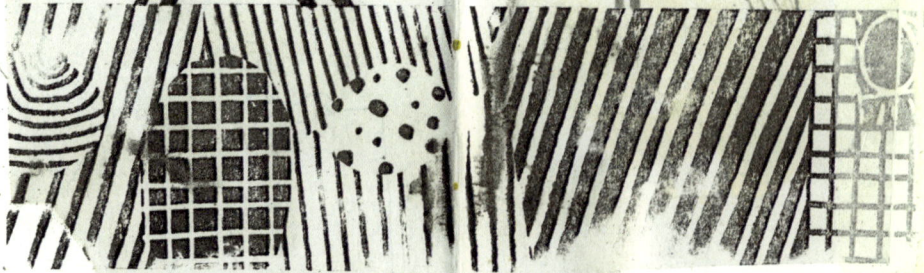

"The poet comes to the studio to show me his latest published work.
He makes a long and impassioned presentation during which I give him my
undivided attention. After turning the last page, he asks me:
—What do you think?
—Did you have fun? I asked, not really knowing what to say.
—Never, he said almost offended. Satisfaction and pleasure are the enemies
of art. Art is the product of pain. Pain is essential. It is essential because it is
necessary and it is essential because it always hurts in the right place."

"—Where does this color come from?
—From the desert.
—And that one?
—From ash.
—And those over there?
—From lichen, from moss, from fear, from the bark of an almond tree, from rosemary, from the cold north wind, from sisal, from broom, from esparto grass, from thirst, from restharrow, from fear, from organza.
—You said fear twice.
—Yes. Because fear is never ending."

"Ever since I discovered, more than 25 years ago, the work of Saul Steinberg, his personality and illustrations have been a familiar presence. I have a good collection of his illustrated books and a couple of beautiful accounts of his thinking: *Reflections and shadows* and *Letters to Aldo Buzzi*.

I often reread fragments on the run of the letters he wrote to his Italian friend. A 54-year long correspondence. I open the book to a random page and savor his pure uncontrived prose. I participate, as much as I can, in the puns and idiomatic acrobatics, and I feel close to many of his ideas. Beyond the modernity and mastery of his illustrations, thanks to these letters I discovered the vulnerable and human man who appreciates details, the attentive and cultivated reader, the mordant nihilist, the critic, the gourmand, the rascal, the traveler, the lover...

At the end of the letter of August 1, 1998, with only a few months to live, Saul Steinberg writes: 'I've been happy for a long time, but I never quite knew it.'

Unlike misery and pain, happiness possesses the gift of discretion. Hysteria is often confused with happiness."

Un-walk

LZF

Music
Miles Davis. *Kind Of Blue.*
John Coltrane. *A Love Supreme.*
Herbert. *Bodily Functions.*

LZF

Sandro Tothill, founder of Luzifer Lamps with Mariví Calvo, met Isidro Ferrer in 2002, at the presentation of Proyecta, a traveling exhibition organized by the Ministry of Foreign Affairs that promoted Spanish design in Latin America. Mariví says that the first thing she thought when she saw his work was that she wanted to work with him.

The first assignment in 2002 was the logo for LZF, her lighting company; the second, twelve years later, involved creating the new communication campaign, with the freedom to do whatever he wanted.

The result in 2015, was Funny Farm, a collection of 18 wooden mischievous-faced characters that stand on two little legs: Atomic Ant, Octo, Grumpy Goat, Mad Mouse, Dolly, Red Rabbit and the rest, made from sapele, Spanish cedar, African ebony, black hyedua, pequia and African padauk.

Over time, some of these animals have become monumental lamps that, despite their grandeur, retain their original simplicity. Funny Farm was made in collaboration with the cabinetmaker Carlos Mur. The lamps were designed using the wood vareta technique in the workshop of the fallero artist Manolo Martín. They won a Goog Design Awards granted by The Chicago Athenaeum, as one of the 100 most remarkable design projects in the world.

"There are far more answers than questions. Everything is overflowing with answers: encyclopedias, newspapers, usage manuals, medical brochures, textbooks, self-help books, speeches, conferences, the TV news, sermons, TED talks, op-ed columns, editorials, advice from friends, councils of ministers, work groups...

The real difficulty doesn't lie in the ability to find adequate answers to the questions but in the opposite, in the formulation of questions that give meaning to the answers.

Questions and answers have independent and differentiated lives but their paths sometimes cross. From these haphazard intersections emerges metaphysics.

Philosophy has numerous responses to very few questions. Religion, on the other hand, provides few and categorical responses to all questions. We call this faith.

Indeed, it can be said that for each question there are hundreds of answers and that each answer doesn't necessarily correspond to a specific question.

Often it's hard to tell the difference between a question and an answer. Answers and questions often switch roles."

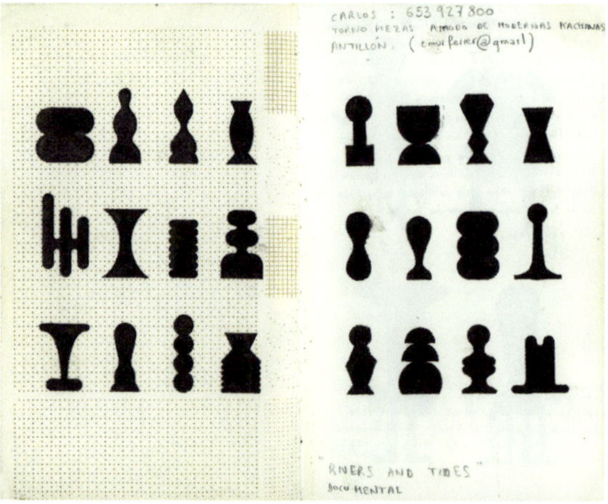

CARLOS : 653 927 800
TORSO MESAS   AMIGOS DE HOSTALES MACHINAS
PASTILLÓN (email@gmail)

"RIVERS AND TIDES"
DOCU-MENTAL

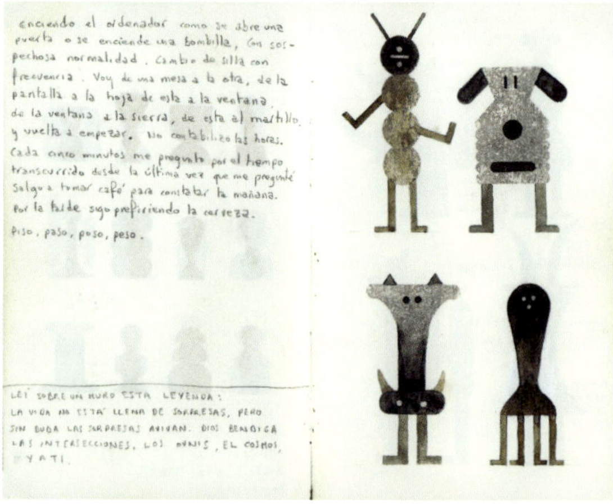

MADERAS   GUATEMA(?)
    POCOBOLO,
    ROJ,
    PERLA
    PALISANDRO
    ROBLE
    NEGRO
    NUTIVE
    TACINO
    GUINGA
    SAPELLI
    NEGRO
    BURINGA
    ENEBRO
PEGAMENTO
B-7EO
ADHESIVO + SPRAY ACTIVADOR

     C

Los sobre un muro esta leyenda:
LA VIDA EN ESTA LLENA DE SORPRESAS, PERO
SIN DUDA LAS SORPRESAS AVISAN. DIOS BENDIGA
LAS INTERSECCIONES, LOS HONES, EL COLMO,
Y A TI.

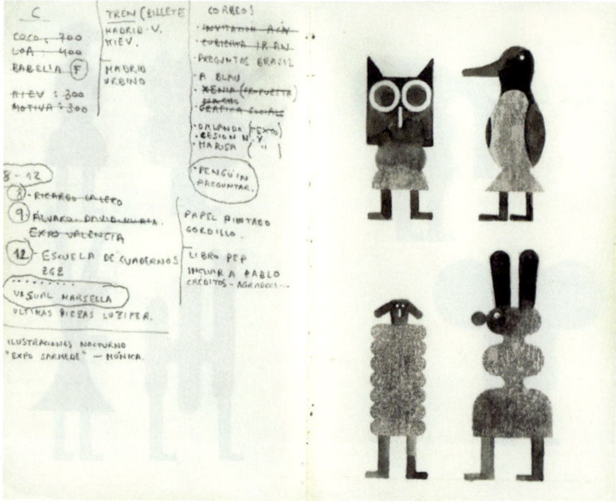

La provincia tiene una parte de resignación
y otra de confianza

"Clarice Lispector said in an interview that she felt like 'literature's guest'. Her answer describes how I feel about design: often I feel like a guest, other times like someone who is stateless, and sometimes like a Martian."

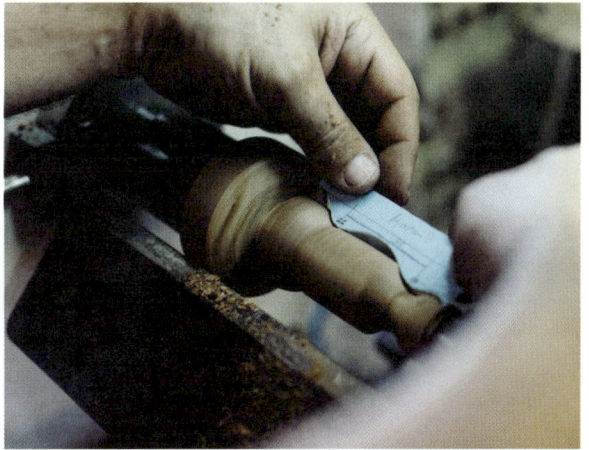

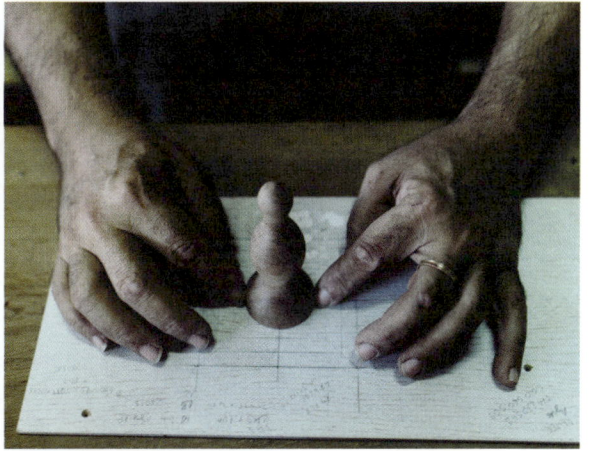

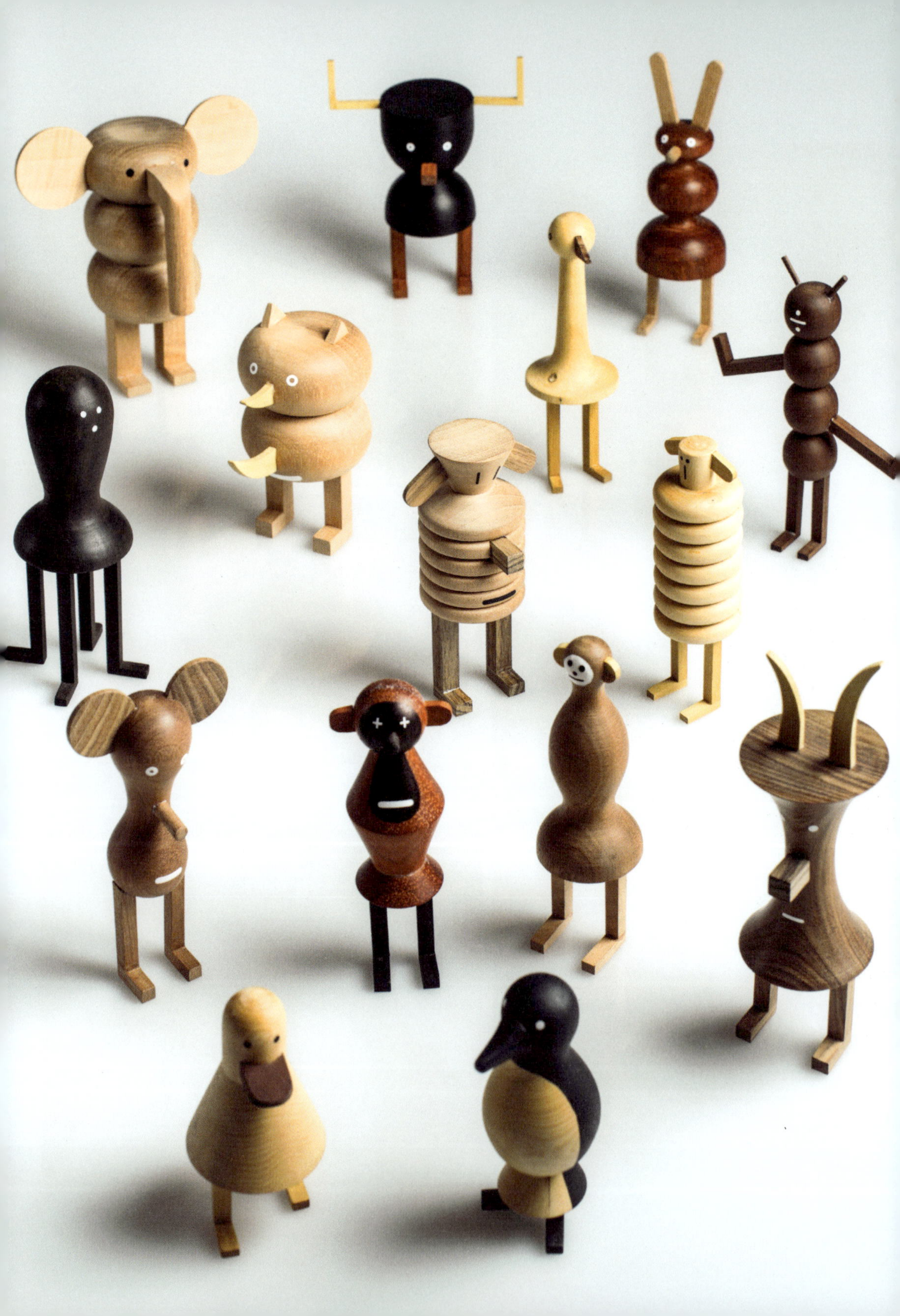

"During the early morning hours, I keep the doors to my studio open: the door that leads directly to the corner between the square and the street and the one, going up a couple of stairs, that connects the studio's inner courtyard to my neighbors' courtyard.

If I stay between these two doors, I can feel a slight breeze.

Along with the noise from the street, some discreet urban wildlife sneaks in, probably seeking refuge from the heat. The spiders have been with me for years. The flies enter in the morning and leave at night. A salamander has taken up residence on the coolest wall of the studio. Yesterday, I surprised an ant crawling across the keyboard to my computer. It was a scout ant. I didn't let him continue because I didn't want him to summon the entire nest. Every day, I collect the cadaver of a cockroach. They die on a strict schedule, almost mathematically, so much so that it arouses a deep curiosity in me. I've begun to develop a funeral ritual.

I usually walk barefoot; sometimes I take off my t-shirt.

Mercedes, my landlady and neighbor, to save herself a few steps, takes advantage of when the doors are open to cut through the inside of the studio. She pokes her head in, asks me if she can, and then slowly crosses the studio. If her hands are full, I help her with the packages. She usually has a story to tell. I know almost all of them. Today, she told me the one about the gigantic Spanish fir in the garden that her father planted when he was a child 120 years ago.

When I go in the kitchen, I step on a dead cockroach that makes a faint crunching sound under my bare foot. I should feel some disgust but am surprised by my absolute indifference. I don't know if I'm getting used to the deaths or to the cockroaches."

"There are questions in this field that are repeated over and over again. One of the most persistent is the one that questions the meaning of this activity. What is design? More than a question it's challenge. There are as many different answers as there are designers.

To repeat the question: What is design?
The range of answers extends from the theory of Terence Conrad, for whom design is a combination of meaning and function, to those of Abraham Moles, who defends the desire of design to intervene in the human environment; to adapt the environment to the needs of individuals or groups of individuals, to more pragmatic views that attribute to design the ability to solve communication problems.

All these definitions are accurate and precise, but they lack poetics.

I like to think of design as making the imaginary possible. To design is to move the realm of the imaginary closer to the domain of the possible.

I'll try to explain. An intentional action always contains an idea, but an idea, by itself, is never enough. To crystallize the utilitarian function of design, the person who designs must make what they imagine possible.

The juncture between the idea and reality is where the designer's work takes place. It's where the battle between the imaginary and what's possible is waged.

The ability to project results is limited by the imagination, However, the technical ability to resolve the matter at hand is what defines the limit of the real. Technique, then, is more than an instrument. It's what prompts and provokes what is real, a way of making possible what remains hidden.

This making possible recovers the Platonic approach that identifies the artisan as 'maker'. Moreover, it confirms, as Henri Bergson, who defined intelligence as the ability to create artificial objects, in particular tools, pointed out, that human identity is based on our condition as *Homo faber.*"

Grumpy Goat
nunca sabe por qué
se enfada y se enfada
porque nunca sabe
por qué se enfada

Grumpy Goat
never knows why
he gets annoyed,
yet he gets annoyed
at the fact that
he doesn't know
why he is annoyed

Photography: María Mira

Octo
ha viajado por todos
los países del mundo menos
por uno; no consigue recordar
cuál le falta

Octo
has traveled to every
country in the world
except one, but he doesn't
remember which one it is

Big Bird
trabaja en un taller
donde fabrican aire
para que los aviones
no se caigan

Big Bird
works at a factory that
makes air so that planes
won't fall out of the sky

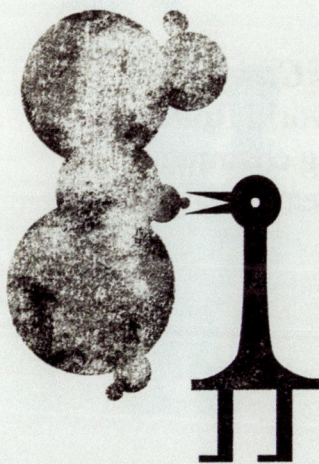

Ronny Rhino
pasa la noche contando
chistes por teléfono
a sus amigos,
son chistes muy viejos

Ronny Rhino
spends his nights
on the phone telling
his friends old jokes that
they've all heard before

Penny Gwin
fue dos veces
consecutivas
campeón mundial de
boxeo sobre ruedas

Penny Gwin
was world Rollerskate
boxing champion
two years in a row

Smelly Fant
se muere de risa
escuchando esas cosas
que dicen los niños
cuando los adultos
han salido de compras

Smelly Fant
laughs like mad
listening to the things kids
say when the grownups
have gone out shopping

New Yorker
está acostumbrado a que
todos le llamen el animal;
le pusieron el apodo
cuando descubrieron que leía

New Yorker
is used to people calling
him "the beast",
they gave him
this nickname when
they discovered
he loved reading

"I see graphic expression as a kind of polyphony, an ensemble of voices and instruments with different timbres, resonances and tones brought together to find the best way to interpret a melody. We could say that graphic design takes into account the peculiarities of different assignments to find the harmonious composition that best suits each one. Each design can be sung in many different ways, but some voices and instruments go together better and uncover unique resonances."

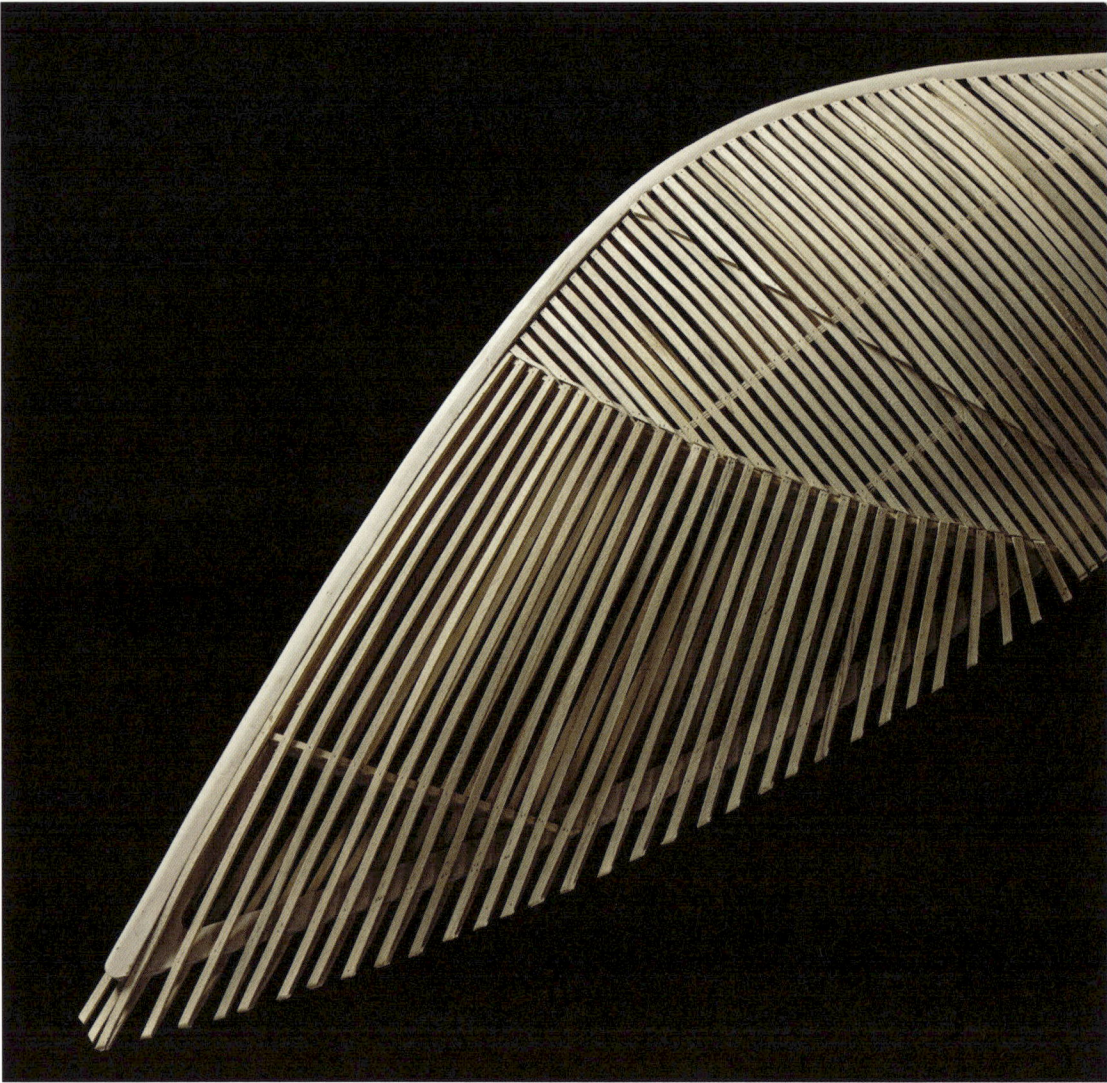

Photography: Santiago Relanzón

Photography: Santiago Relanzón (left), Emilio Lekuona (right)

"I consider time to be an important and substantial part of every creative process. Time to observe, to discover, to experiment, to reflect, to act; a time to let things unfold on their own, a time to allow things to be what they want to be. I try to incorporate time into my designs."

Photography: Cualiti & María Mira

"Just before leaving on a trip, I received in an envelope *The Pillow Book*, which I had lent to someone before summer. This is the fourth time it has come to me unexpectedly. It's book of notes written by Sei Shonagon in the 10th century that contains a detailed record of wonders. The first time, I came to it through Borges. This was when Latin American literature in general, but Cortazar and Borges especially, was a mainstay of my reading.
Along with María Kodama, Borges translated this book directly from the Japanese.

The second time, it entered my radar through the poetic prose of Christian Bobin. He referred to its lists in the final pages of *Un assassin blanc comme neige (A Murderer So White as Snow)*. The third time, it appeared suddenly in *Sans soleil (Sunless)*, the documentary film by Chris Marker. Too many coincidences to be overlooked. On this trip, the book is part of my luggage.

Sei Shonagon was fascinated by lists: 'list of elegant things', 'distressing things', or 'things that aren't worth doing'. One day, he prepared the list of 'things that make your heart race'. In the middle of the ocean, at 40,000 feet, I think about what is required to make one's heart beat faster, in the adjectives needed to make this happen.

Chris Marker states that naming should be enough. 'For us, a sun isn't a complete sun unless it's radiant, and a spring isn't a spring unless it's crystal clear. In Japanese poetry, using adjectives is as crass as leaving the price tag on a gift. There's a way to say boat, rock, cloud, frog, crow, hail, heron and chrysanthemum that includes adjectives.'

I long to use images the way Japanese poetry uses words. I read somewhere that 'to read is to add'. If this is true, it means that to write is to remove. I like literature, art and design that eschew everything unnecessary, that eliminate what is superfluous."

Photography: Cualiti

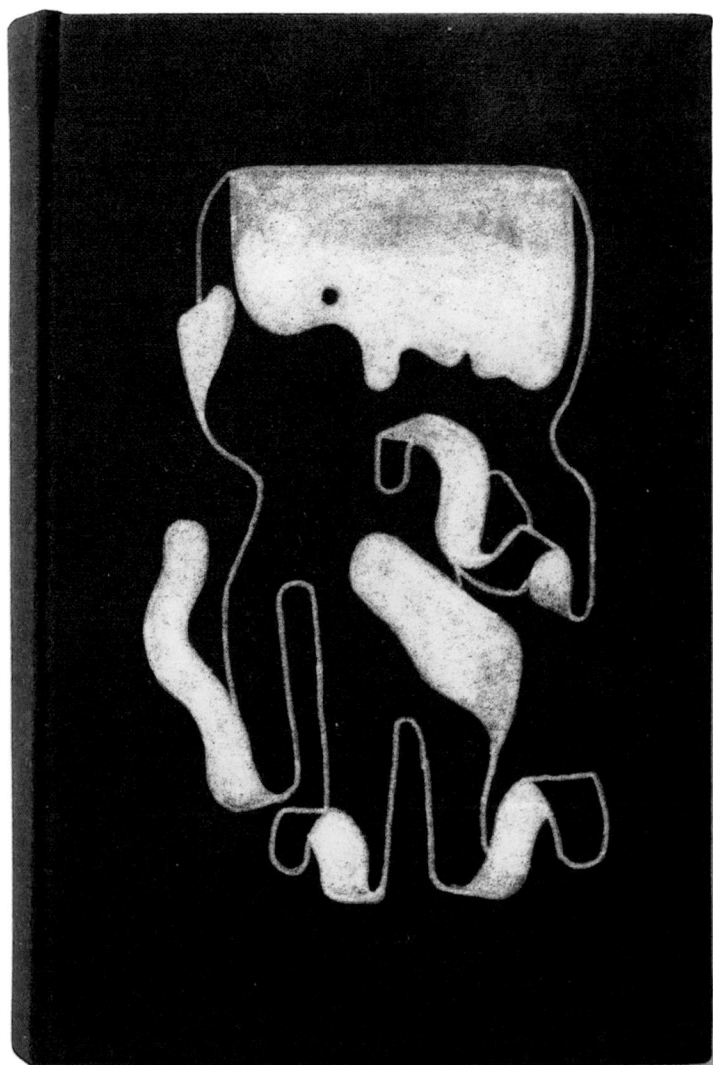

Un-investigate

LIBRO DE OTRO

Music
Moondog. *Moondog. 1969, Moondog 2. 1971.*

LIBRO DE OTRO

Libro de otro (Other book) is a personal and unpublished project that Isidro Ferrer began in 2020.

It's a project tied to conceptualism, to the *ready made* and to some ideas that emerged in the seventies about the reuse of preexisting elements in which he recovers some of the principles of the mediated book and the non-book in order to experiment on the book object as if it were a palimpsest. Isidro Ferrer proposes the de-territorialization of the already published object –and therefore restricted to the borders that its condition imposes– in order to inhabit it and transform it into a different object.

"Design is a hybrid language, the fruit of a sum of knowledge, techniques and expressions that enables and seeks perpetual movement. Searching is a must. I search and, more often than not, what I find I find by accident or by a stroke of *luck*, and I continue searching. Searching compels me."

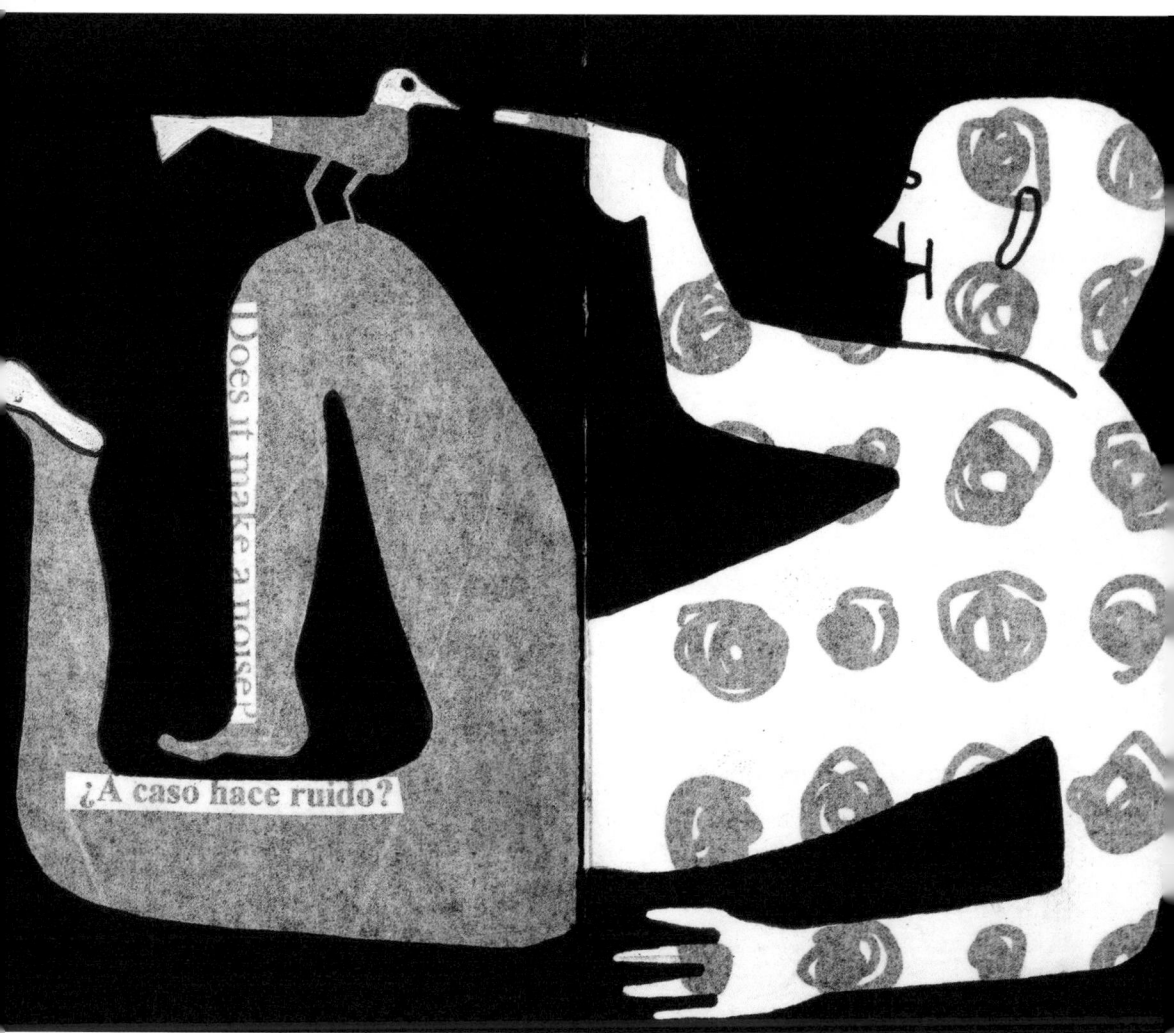

Does it make a noise?

¿A caso hace ruido?

"Signs in the sky, under the sign of the stars, in coffee grounds, fate, destiny, trace, track, the sign of the times, lit signs, smoke signals, gestures, poses, the lines on the palm, furrows in the ground, chance or fortune.

Signs.

A sign is an object, phenomenon or action that conventionally replaces another. A sign is a signal. It's also the minimum unit of expression made up of a signifier and a signified.

A sign is the expression of an idea or a thought.

A sign is the trail I leave behind in my travels, and signs are the signals that help me move through the world.

I point with my finger, at something or someone, in order to identify it. A sign informs and through it, we are able to communicate. The gestures, the movements that accompany words are signs, sometimes with greater significance than these.

A sign is also an indication".

MAT
AMO
MA
ELL
IRR
SON

"As a child, when I was sick and couldn't go to school, time stood still in the reduced space of my bedroom. The half-lowered blind let in the light, projecting narrow strips of sunlight onto the bed and the wall, tinting the minutes with ocher.

I would watch the dust descend slowly between the chiaroscuro of the blind. They appeared and disappeared between light and shadow. Now yes, now no. I tried to guess the path a single mote of dust would take from its appearance through the highest strip of light until it got lost at the limits of the bed.

I was aware that it was impossible to distinguish one mote from another. I knew that only my imagination could isolate that one small silvery mote I had chosen to describe its path between the sky and my bedroom floor from the others. The light, cold tile floor. That returned me to reality when my bare feet touched its cold surface. The bed was my private universe. Anything could happen in it; everything fit. The entire world between the folds in the sheets.

In the afternoon my fever would rise. My mother would seat on the bed beside me caressing my head. When she wasn't close to me, I could feel her singing in the kitchen, a muffled sound like an old gramophone. I listened to those melodies even then through the muted sound of nostalgia. My mother's singing was the reassurance of her existence. And also of mine."

COLORES

EL BLANCO Y EL NEGRO
NO ESTÁN INCLUIDOS EN
EL ESPECTRO DEL COLOR
PERO PARA MÍ
SON COLORES
Y SI SE CANCEL
MÁXIMO CONTRASTE
Y EL MÁXIMO CONTRASTE
ES LA MÁXIMA BRAVEZA. MI
ESFUERZO PARA LOGRAR
EL CONTRASTE MÁXIMO.
ROSA Y VERDE
LA COLOCACION DE
COLORES UNO SOBRE
EL C
ESTO DEPENDE DE
LA RELACION
LA PROPORCIÓN
EL RITMO
EL TAMAÑO.
LA CANTIDAD
Y CÓMO COLOCAMOS
COLORES JUNTOS
ESTO SE DA
A LA MUERTE

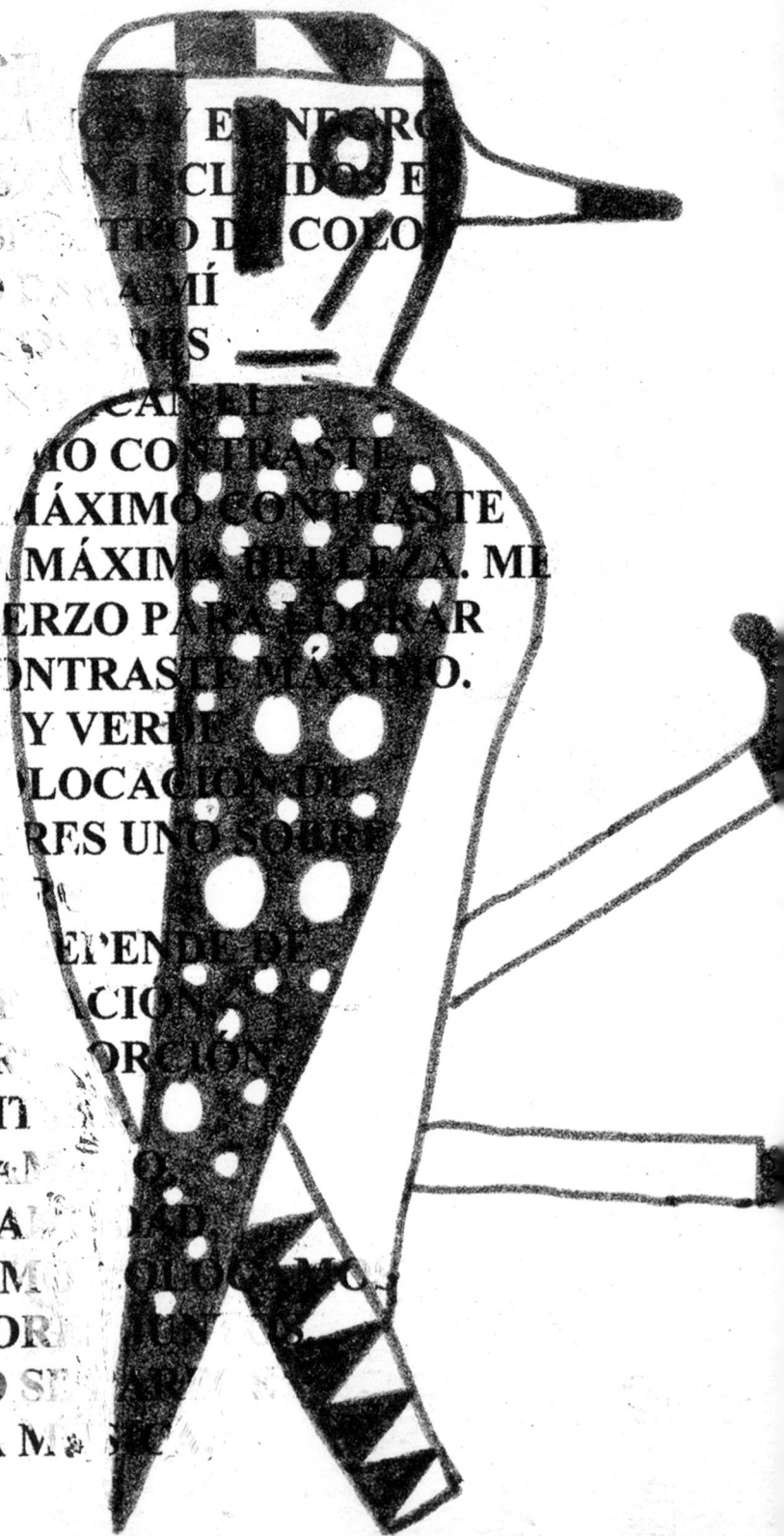

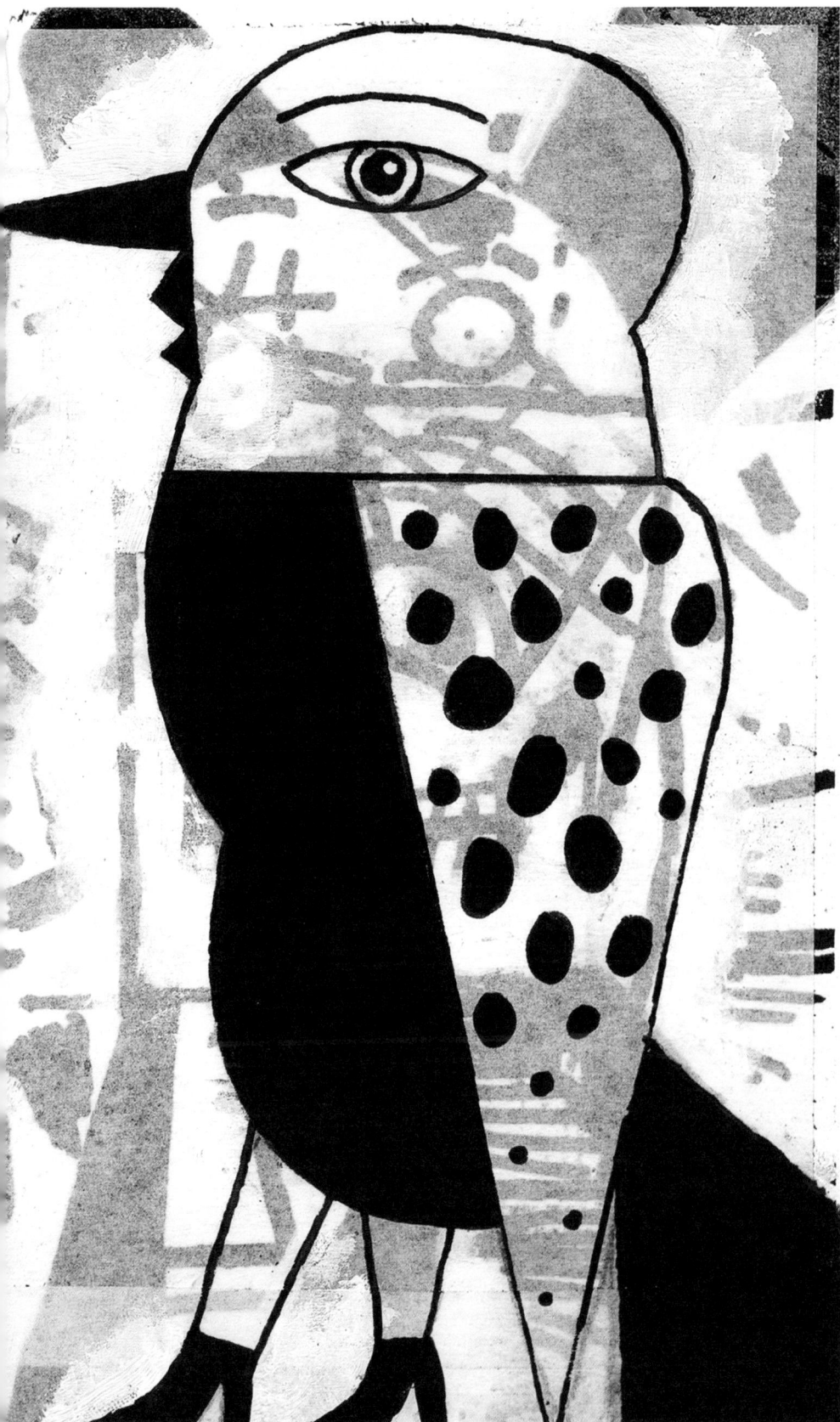

Un-arrange

CAHIER DE VACANCES

Music
Henri Salvador. *Chambre avec vue.*

CAHIER DE VACANCES

In 2013, the Fondation Marseille-Provence commissioned Isidro Ferrer to design the young audiences communication program for the Marseille European Capital of Culture celebration.
They explicitly asked him to do more than simply provide information about the programed activities. In addition, they wanted him to create a playful and participatory object that would encourage children and adults to navigate their way through the program,
Avoiding educational or training requirements, he proposed a booklet that, like a travel journal, is a wild open space for play where everything is possible, inviting the reader to create and interact with unprecedented worlds.
As Grassa Toro, author of the texts, describes it: "It isn't a notebook designed for a vacation. It's a notebook to make it a vacation when you want it to be a vacation."

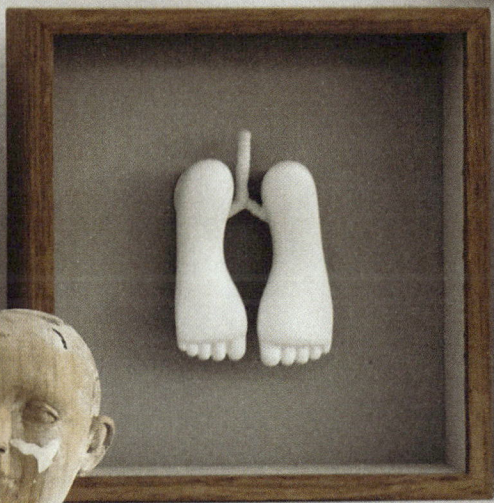

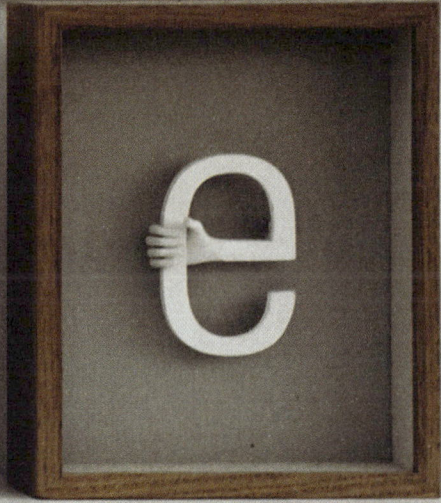

"I travel constantly, more than ever, from one place to another. I like this chance passage, where I almost never decide where or how. I like feeling like a stranger, not being the master of my steps, to go where my feet take me without putting up any resistance. I like being a stranger in an unknown place. I like to be unknown and not knowing. It means starting over again and again."

"I'm interested in objects and their meaning and symbolic value. Their material and formal qualities also interest me. An object is form and function. Form proceeds from function but transcends it. It is even capable of becoming independent of it.

Through our actions, we can change the shape and meaning of things. I like this game of transformation and metamorphosis where everything is what it is and nothing is what it seems.

Recycling helps with this transformation, but in itself it doesn't interest me very much. I don't strive to use antique or beautiful things for their plastic qualities but to use material with meaning that leads to a displacement of perception.

Recovering and recycling useless objects by changing their nature can be the way, but often it's better to start from scratch, building the object anew to reveal its hidden meaning.

In this sense, the assemblage is not an end. It's a means that allows me, in the manner of Josep Renau with his use of collage, to reveal paradoxes."

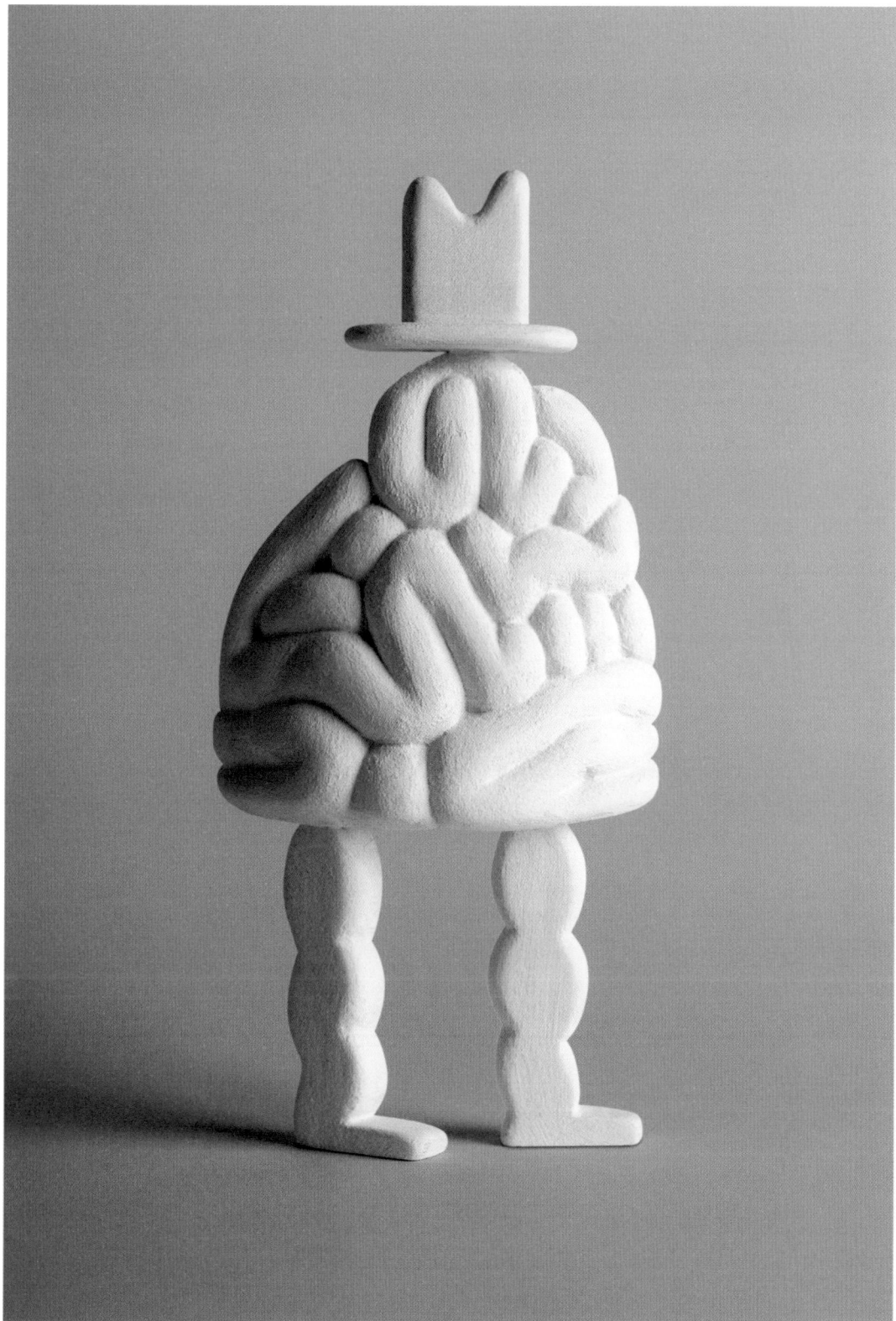

"The first time I heard of Dieter Roth's existence it hit me like a flood. Nicolás Sánchez called to convince me to visit the Dieter Roth exhibition with him at the Barcelona Museum of Contemporary Art. His enthusiasm was infectious. We planned the trip down to the letter but, two days before we were supposed to leave, something unexpected prevented me from joining him. I asked him to bring me back the catalog of the exhibition.

A catalog existed but Nicolás didn't have enough money to buy one. Instead, he bought a school notebook and like a good student, took notes.
Armed with a pencil, a whole lot of patience and a method to his credit, he constructed his own thoughtful catalog on graph paper as he toured the museum. He copied each and every one of the pieces assembled in the rooms. He drew a detailed map of the route and the layout of the works, including brief footnotes of his own impressions. Brief, according to him, so as not to overly influence my reading.

Where the mastery of the graphic account became blurry, Nicolás embellished it with a description of what happened. On his return, not only did I admire the pieces in the exhibit, but I was also able to enjoy them together with Nicolás' written impressions.

This personalized catalog has become, over time, one of the most frequently consulted books in my library. A few days later, out of curiosity, I ordered the actual exhibition catalog by mail. Needless to say, I kept the original copy."

Mets en désordre cette image pour qu'elle
devienne très ennuyeuse.

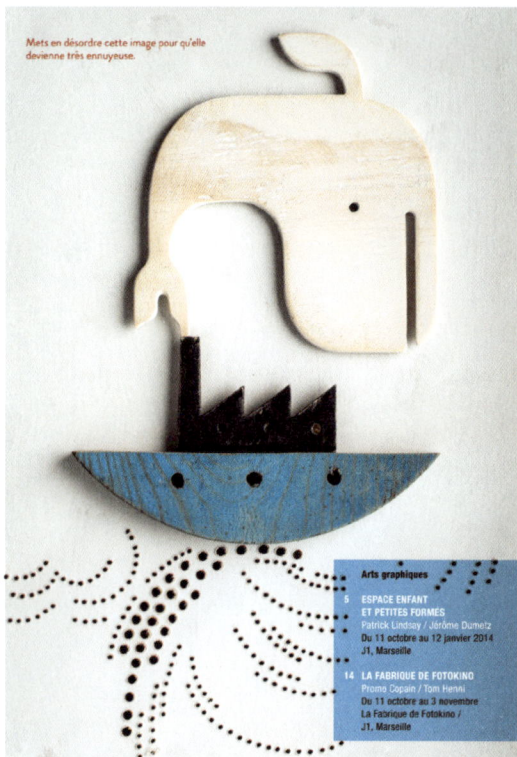

Écris la conversation entre Paul,
l'insecte froid et Pal, l'insecte chaud.

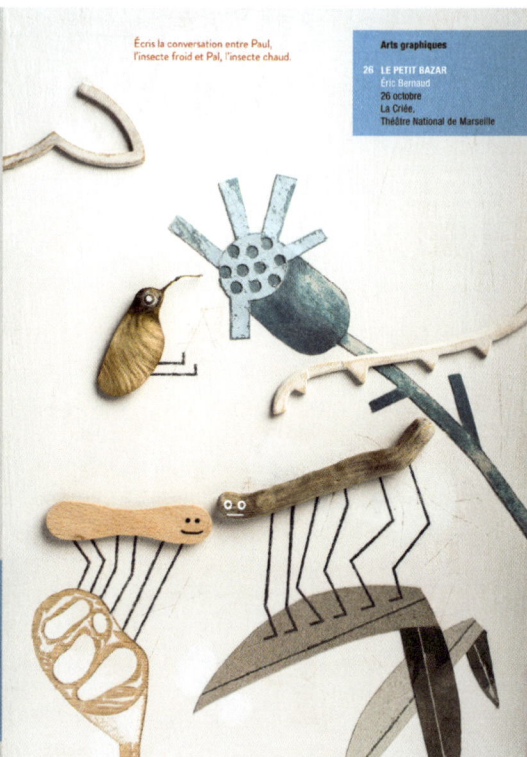

Arts graphiques

26 **LE PETIT BAZAR**
Éric Bernaud
26 octobre
La Criée.
Théâtre National de Marseille

Arts graphiques

5 **ESPACE ENFANT
ET PETITES FORMES**
Patrick Lindsay / Jérôme Dumetz
Du 11 octobre au 12 janvier 2014
J1, Marseille

14 **LA FABRIQUE DE FOTOKINO**
Promo Copain / Tom Henni
Du 11 octobre au 3 novembre
La Fabrique de Fotokino /
J1, Marseille

Lequel des trois cyclistes de l'équipe Bauhaus ne verra pas
les vaches sur le bord de la route ?

Essaie d'atteindre la maison sans que le loup n'entende tes pas.

Exposition / LES EXPÉDITIONS IMAGINAIRES

4 **L'île extraordinaire des Robinsons**
Du 26 octobre au 4 janvier 2014
Alcazar, Marseille

Le fabuleux musée des songes
Du 25 octobre au 4 janvier 2014
Médiathèque George Sand, Vitrolles

À l'abordage !
Du 12 octobre au 11 janvier 2014
Marseille, Rousset, Velaux,
Saint-Martin-de-Crau, Meyreuil,
Châteauneuf-les-Martigues

Conte

8 **LES CONTES DE LA MÉMÉ**
Katia Poliès
16 octobre
Bibliothèque municipale Jorgi Reboul,
Septèmes-les-Vallons

16 **LE MARATHON DU MERVEILLEUX**
Laurent Daycard
20 octobre
La Baleine qui dit « Vagues », Marseille

20 **LE GRAND BAZAR...**
Weepers circus
23 octobre
Théâtre des Salins, Martigues

Découpe une de ces mains
et dis au revoir aux bateaux qui partent.

Place chaque pensée dans la tête qui la pense.

Trouve les 0'7 différences.

Habille le génie avec un costume
de vendredi d'automne.

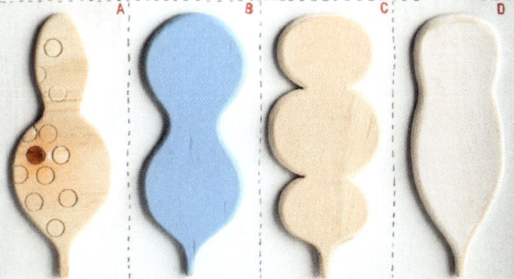

I dreamed

"I dreamed I was an architect and that I had to design a city, a new city. I knew I couldn't do it because I was an outsider to the subject.
In the non-existent city where I had to work, there were only one hotel and large abandoned avenues. The hotel was filled with people. I had lost my luggage and the models of the buildings I was supposed to build. I had improvised the models out of scattered pieces of cardboard.
I was supposed to present my designs to a committee.
The only inhabitants of the city lived crowded together in this place.
I tried to find a way to avoid meeting anyone in the halls. I had to go up and down the freight elevator that was so narrow barely half a person fit inside. Shut up in a room overlooking a field of vacant lots, I was going over and over my models and the projects I had to present. All night long I was entangled in a job that isn't even mine."

Souffle pour que la chaussure sèche
ou pour qu'il arrête de pleuvoir.

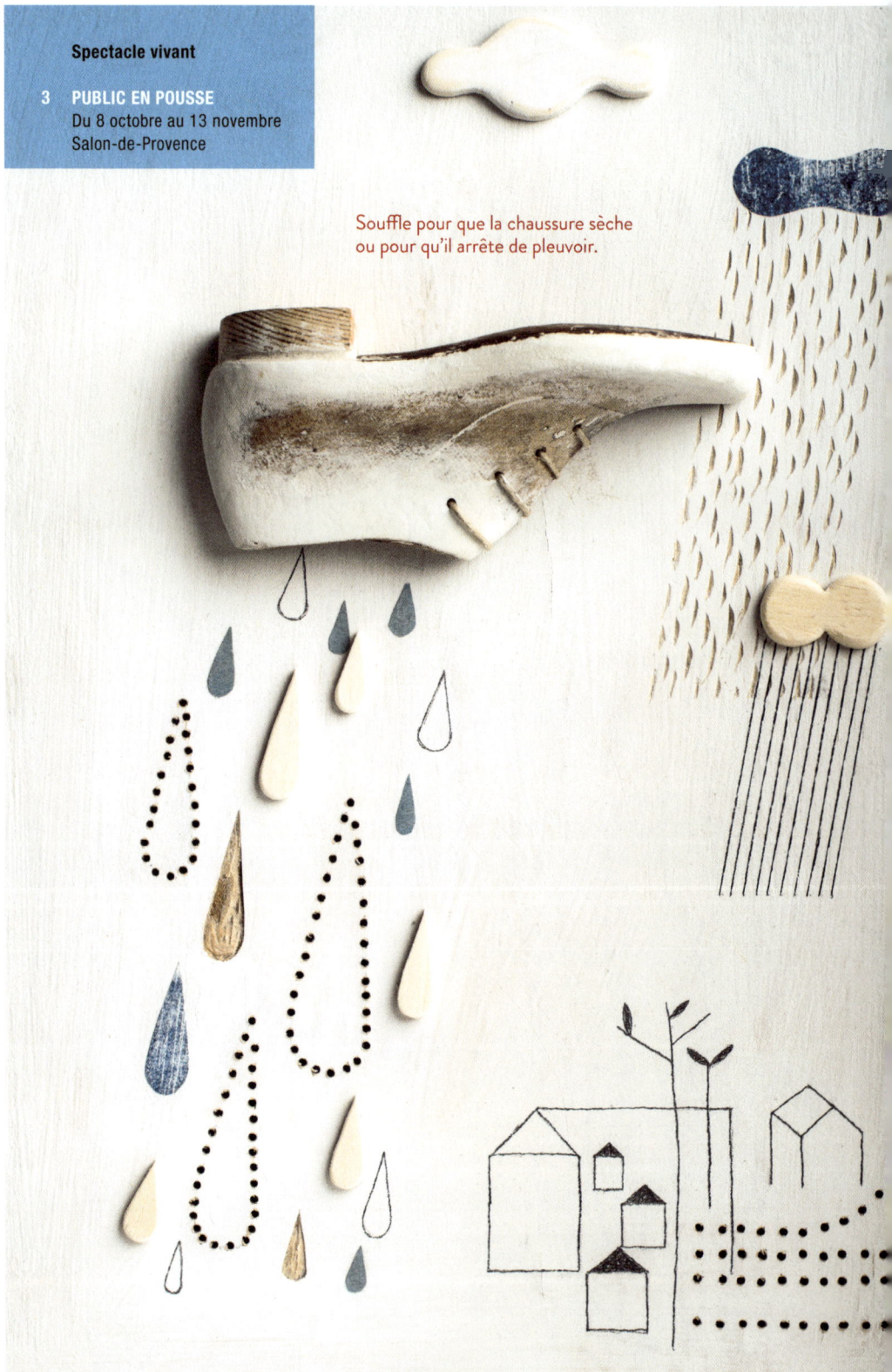

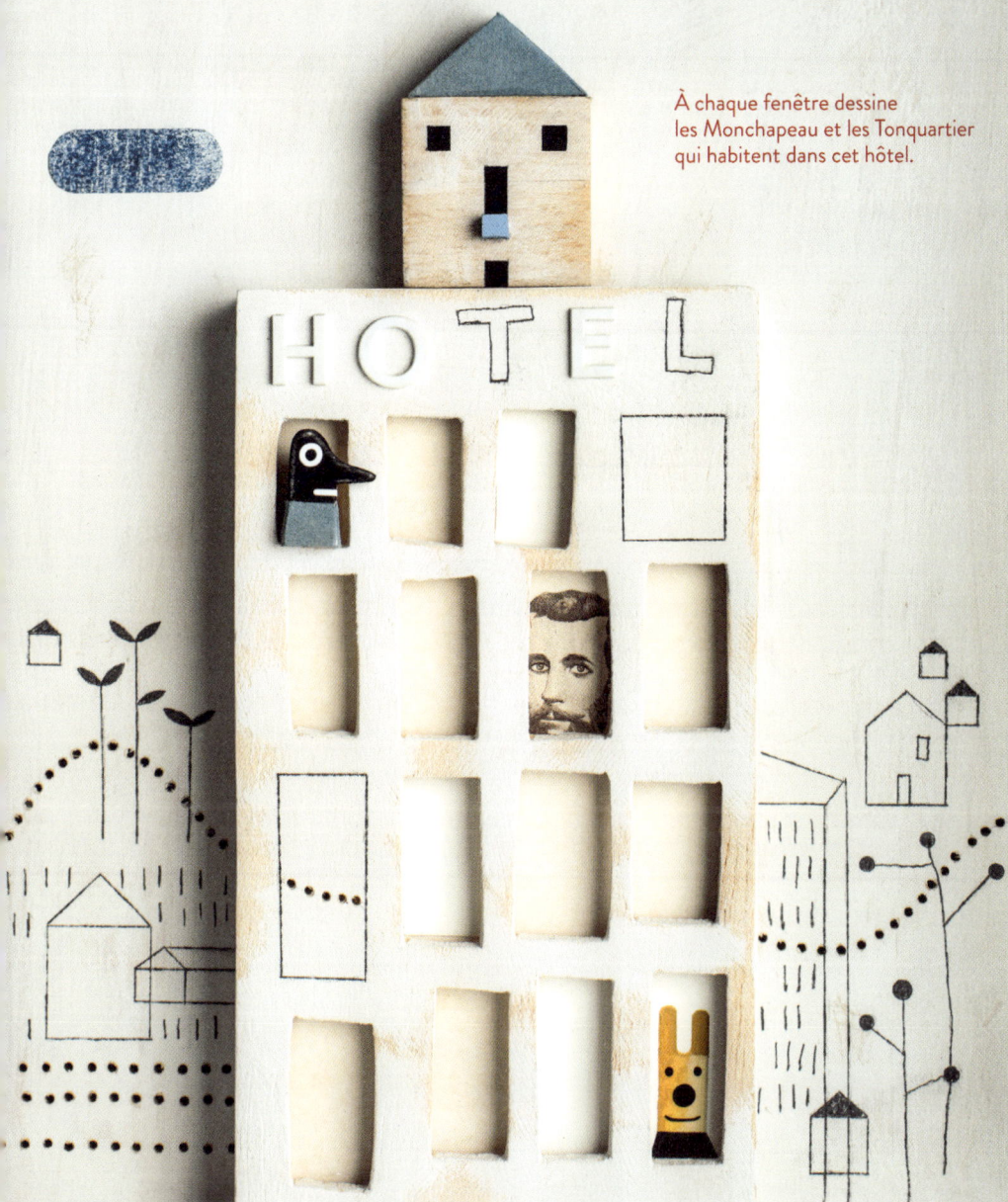

À chaque fenêtre dessine
les Monchapeau et les Tonquartier
qui habitent dans cet hôtel.

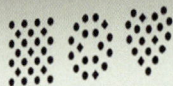

C° CAHIER
de
VACANCES

"The Greeks didn't know anything about blue. For them, the color blue was something so natural it didn't need a name.

The sea, the sky, the horizon are blue because of the accumulation of emptinesses and transparencies. Nothing upon nothing."